W9-BZT-403

"Take a close look at *Java Design: Building Better Apps and Applets.* The subject of the book is design, not just Java programming. It's about choosing better design strategies inspired by the intrinsic language features found in Java. The strategies in this book apply to any design, even when the target language is something other than Java. Lots of helpful insights; the chapters on 'Design with Interfaces' and 'Design with Threads' are especially good."

—*Roger Smith, Software Development Magazine*

"Coad and Mayfield's book offers a solid introduction to Java set in the context of good design practice, with a particularly insightful treatment of message interfaces."

—*David Taylor, "Object Technology,*
A Manager's Guide" (Second Edition)

"This is a revolutionary book in the Java programming book market since it doesn't teach you how to program . . . This is a book for those who need to implement large and complex applications and want to learn how to use all the powerful mechanisms offered by the language in order to create better and well-organized applications."

—*from a review in Java Universe Developer*

"Just finished devouring Java Design and I loved it! I think it is one of those books that will influence my thinking for years to come. (And there have only been a few other books like it in my experience)."

—*John Pinto, Director of R&D,*
Precision Programming, Inc.

"I have been a procedural coder for the last 10 years and within the last year, have started getting my feet wet in Java. I quickly realized the importance of having more knowledge on OOP methodology but the books that I acquired were fairly dry . . . [Then] I stumbled across your book . . . I knew I was hooked after the first couple of pages and have since read it numerous times. Thank you very much for providing such a high caliber product; I'm looking forward to your future work. I just purchased your other title *Object Models: Strategies, Patterns, and Applications* and am looking forward to that one as well. Thanks once again."

—*Ilan Berci, DSP Engineer, Voxware*

ISBN 0-13-911181-6

90000

9 780139 111815

"I am reading your book entitled *Java Design: Building Better Apps and Applets*. I am using many of the techniques you described in the book and it has really helped me nail down the design of my application."

—Greg Bondy, Advisory Software Engineer, IBM

"To Peter Coad and Mark Mayfield, let me say that *Java Design: Building Better Apps and Applets* is a terrific book, and written in a refreshingly clear style. I appreciate all that you are doing to help us all make our programs work better."

—Tony Coates, Multimedia Developer, Educational Multimedia Services, The University of Queensland, Brisbane, Australia

"To be a good Java programmer, you need to be a good object-oriented programmer. And you need to understand the way the building materials of a language like Java shape application design. Peter Coad does. He's an object-oriented programming guru, whose firm, Object International (www.oi.com), has been engaged in many object-oriented projects in many industries. He brings a wealth of experience to an analysis of Java from a software designer's standpoint. He knows how messy, brittle, and ugly design starts, and he shows us how to use Java to nip it in the bud. He identifies some basic patterns that maximize clean, flexible, reusable design. He stresses the use of composition over inheritance. Coad is not big on inheritance: he's seen it misused a lot, and he sets forth clear and limiting criteria for its use. He shows good Java-based ways to compose objects with other objects, preserving encapsulation and expanding flexibility. He also shows intelligent strategies for using interfaces. In my own current Java projects, Coad and Mayfield's book made a lot of design issues clearer. It has sent me back to the drawing board, but with a much more well-rounded design sensibility. This is an excellent book for a beginning object-oriented programmer starting out with Java. It makes clear the appropriate use of interfaces, and points out the pitfalls of multiple inheritance and a number of other practices . . . I strongly recommend this book. Anyone who has learned Java's basics but wants to know how to put them together to do good design should buy it."

—John Stoner, Reviewer, Chicagoland Java User's Group

"I read with great pleasure your new book. Being an enthusiastic Java programmer, I really appreciated your excellent combination of OO design principles and Java concepts like interfaces."

—Harald Nekvasil, TAB Ltd.

"I'd like to take this opportunity to praise your book *Java Design: Building Better Apps and Applets*. I spend a *lot* of money on books, and really appreciate when a book is *easy* to justify based on its content."

—Mike Thomas

Java Design

Building Better Apps and Applets

2nd edition

Peter Coad and

Mark Mayfield

with Jonathan Kern

To subscribe to the Coad Letter®, visit:
www.oi.com

To join a Prentice Hall PTR Internet mailing list, point to:
www.prenhall.com/register

YOURDON PRESS
PRENTICE-HALL BUILDING
Upper Saddle River, NJ 07458
http://www.phptr.com

Selected Titles from the
YOURDON PRESS COMPUTING SERIES

Ed Yourdon, *Advisor*

From Peter Coad

To David Thomas Coad
My very loving son

From Mark Mayfield

To Casey Lee Mayfield
My inquisitive one

Library of Congress Cataloging-in-Publication Data

Coad, Peter.

    JAVA design: building better apps and applets / Peter Coad, Mark
Mayfield. – 2nd ed.

       p.   cm. – (Yourdon Press computing series)

    Includes index.

    ISBN 0-13-911181-6 (pbk.)

    1. Java (Computer program language)   I. Mayfield, Mark.
II. Title.   III. Series.

QA76.73.J38C65   1999

005.13'3–dc21   98-48514

                                             CIP

Editorial Production: *Precision Graphic Services, Inc.*
Acquisitions Editor: *Jeffrey Pepper*
Manufacturing Manager: *Alexis R. Heydt*
Marketing Manager: *Dan Rush*
Cover Design Director: *Jerry Votta*
Cover Design: *Anthony Gemmellaro*

Published by Prentice Hall PTR
Prentice-Hall, Inc.
A Simon & Schuster Company
Upper Saddle River, NJ 07458

Java™, JavaBeans™, and Enterprise Beans ™, are trademarks of Sun Microsystems, Inc.
Together®, Together/J®,and Together/C++® are registered trademarks
of Object International Software Ltd.
The Coad Letter® is a registered trademark of Object International, Inc.

The publisher offers discounts on this book when ordered
in bulk quantities. For more information, contact:

Corporate Sales Department
Prentice-Hall PTR
1 Lake Street
Upper Saddle River, NJ 07458
Phone: 800-382-3419
FAX: 201-236-7141
E-mail: corpsales@prenhall.com

Printed in the United States of America
10 9 8 7 6 5 4 3 2

ISBN 0-13-911181-6

Prentice-Hall International (UK) Limited, *London*
Prentice-Hall of Australia Pty. Limited, *Sydney*
Prentice-Hall Canada, Inc., *Toronto*
Prentice-Hall Hispanoamericana S.A., *Mexico*
Prentice-Hall of India Private Limited, *New Delhi*
Prentice-Hall of Japan, Inc., *Tokyo*
Simon & Schuster Asia Pte. Ltd., *Singapore*
Editora Prentice-Hall do Brasil, Ltda., *Rio de Janeiro*

Contents

Chapter 3

Design with Interfaces 81

Chapter 4

Design with Threads   **173**

Chapter 5

Design with Notification   223

Acknowledgments

Special thanks to our friends and colleagues who inspire, encourage, and expect the best from us. We especially appreciate their advice, feedback, and support during the development of this book:

Don Baldwin
Frank Baker
Chuck Garon
Dietrich Charisius
Jeff De Luca
David E. DeLano
Peter Durcansky
Michael Gerasimov
Ray Haygood
J.D. Hildebrand
Tatsuya Hirooka
Fyodor Isakov
Kazuyuki Ishibashi
Shingo Kamiya
Dmitri Krasnov
Rich Lemieux
Michael Mannion
Jill Nicola
Scott Oaks
Nikolai Puntikov
J. Kyle Rickett
Hanspeter Siegrist

Erik Stein
Frank Sterkmann
Paul Týma
Mats Weidmar

with very special thanks to Andy Carmichael, David North, Stephen
Palmer, and Mike Swainston-Rainford.

Preface
to the Second Edition

It's been two years since the writing of the first edition of *Java Design*. Java is growing up nicely and is gaining widespread acceptance in many industries around the globe. All of our workshops and mentoring are with Java projects now, an exciting transition from the "just getting started" times of two short years ago.

In the first edition, we set out to write a book on design rather than programming. We did this for several reasons. One, we are designers at heart; we architect and shape large software systems for a living and truly love what we do. Two, we realize that there are hundreds (and hundreds) of Java programming books today—and that we have little to add to that genre. Three, we seek to write books that have lasting value, and so, did our best to insulate valuable design content from the evolution of Java and related technologies.

The first edition has stood the test of time. While some Java programming books have gone through as many as four editions, Java Design has continued as a best-seller for two years running.

The biggest visual change is the second edition's complete transition to UML notation. We've worked with UML (currently version 1.2) for some time now on real projects. We've looked for ways to use it more effectively, still communicating some of the subtleties of earlier notations. More and more readers have asked for us to make this move. In this edition we do so.

The biggest content change is the second edition's many new sections, 68 pages of new material, delivering:

- Eight new "design with interfaces" strategies (Chapter 3)

    1. Design-in: common features

    2. Design-in: role doubles

    3. Design-in: behavior across roles

    4. Design-in: collections and members

    5. Design-in: common interactions

    6. Design-in: intra-class roles

    7. Design-in: plug-in algorithms

    8. Design-in: feature sequences

- How to design a "responsible thread," one that knows when it can safely terminate itself (Chapter 4)

- How to use inner classes to encapsulate interface adapters (Chapter 5)

- Five additional notification mechanisms (Chapter 5)

    1. Source-listener

    2. Source-support-listener (JavaBeans-style notification)

    3. Producer-bus-consumer (InfoBus-style notification)

    4. Model-view-controller (Swing-style notification)

    5. Source-listener across a network (Enterprise JavaBeans-style notification)

We hope you enjoy this new material as much as we have enjoyed developing it in practice.

Thank you to each of you who have taken the time to write with feedback, suggestions, kind words, and gentle nudges. We value you and your input.

Yours for better design,

Peter Coad
President, Object International, Inc.
coad@oi.com   www.oi.com

Mark Mayfield
Senior Object-Model Architect, Net Explorer., Inc.
mmayfield@netexplorer.com www.netexplorer.com

Why Java Design?

Building materials profoundly affect design techniques.

Home construction materials affect home design. Fabrics affect clothing design. And yes, programming construction materials (languages) affect software design.

In every field of human endeavor, new construction materials are followed by new design methods; hence, "design with Java."

From a designer's perspective, it's worth taking a closer look at Java. What new building materials will it give us? How will these materials affect the way we think about, discuss, trade off, and improve our designs?

Java was designed to *prevent* common mistakes in object-oriented design and programming, especially C++ design and programming.

Java design is profound. It has forever changed how we think about object models and scenarios. It makes object models and scenario views pluggable—unplug an object from one class; plug in an object from another class; and continue on your way, as long as both classes implement the needed interface. This is very significant indeed.

Design

Chapter 1 delivers a practical "how-to" guide for effective design. It introduces a business example and a real-time example that wind their way through the entire book.

> Design by Example
>
> > Identify purpose and features
> >
> > Select classes
> >
> > Sketch a user interface
> >
> > Work out dynamics with scenarios
> >
> > Build an object model

If you are well-versed in object-oriented design, you may choose to scan Chapter 1 and then proceed with Chapter 2.

Java-Inspired Design

Chapter 2 establishes that composition is the norm, inheritance is the exception; composition is more flexible, inheritance is more rigid; composition is more encapsulated; inheritance is only somewhat encapsulated. It points out a fivefold checklist for deciding when it's a good idea to use inheritance, and (more often) when it's a good idea to avoid it.

> Design with Composition, Rather than Inheritance
>
> > Composition: the norm
> >
> > Inheritance: the exception (and its risks)

Inheritance vs. interfaces

Five "must satisfy" criteria

Chapter 3 presents the most significant aspects of Java-inspired design: freedom from object connections that are hardwired to just one class of objects and freedom from scenario interactions that are hardwired to just one class of objects. For systems in which flexibility, extensibility, and pluggability are key issues, Java-style interfaces are a must. Indeed, the larger the system and the longer the potential life span of a system the more significant interface–centric design becomes.

Design with Interfaces

Factor-out interfaces

Repeaters

Proxies

Analogous apps

Future expansion

Design-in Interfaces

Common features

Role doubles

Behavior across roles

Collections and members

Common interactions

Intra-class roles

Plug-in methods

Plug-in feature sequences

Chapter 4 brings out when to use concurrency and how to use it safely. Most designs must account for multiple streams of program execution; this chapter shows how to do that safely. Threads give you a system-level, simple way to provide concurrent execution paths that can be prioritized to handle your main tasks and your lower priority auxiliary tasks.

Design with Threads

How; why; when to avoid; how long

Sync: what's guaranteed, what's not

Shared value (and keeping out of trouble)

Shared resource (and keeping out of trouble)

Multiple clients, multiple threads within an object

Multiple thread objects, multiple threads within an object

Interface adapters

Chapter 5 examines how one object notifies others about a significant change. Passive notification is simple yet resource intensive. Timer-based notification is a useful pattern, yet active notification is the most interesting choice. This is an essential ingredient for problem–domain object reuse; it's an essential ingredient for designing loosely-coupled subsystems. Java's own active notification mechanism (observable-observer) is defective; this chapter goes beyond its weaknesses, showing you how to really get the job done.

Design with Notification

Observable-observer

Source-listener

Source-support-listener (JavaBeans-style notification)

Produce-bus-consumer (InfoBus-style notification)

Passive, time-based, active

Three appendices follow Chapter 5: Design Strategies, Notation Summary, and Java Visibility.

A Design Book

We love Java programming. It's contagious, way cool, and lots of fun.

But that is not the subject of this book.

This book is about design. Indeed, it is about better design strategies that were inspired by the intrinsic language features found in Java.

These strategies may be applied in any design, even if the target language is not Java.

Java snippets, short and to-the-point examples and excerpts, appear throughout this book. They include lots of comments, so you can read along and understand the design issue, even without prior experience with Java.

Eventually, you might want to read a programming book on Java. We own a stack of them! Our personal favorites to date are

> Cornell, Gary, and Horstmann, Cay: *Core Java*.
> Prentice Hall.
> This programming book has a good blend of illustrations and source code. It includes quite a bit of material on threads too.

> Flanagan, David: *Java in a Nutshell*. O'Reilly
> & Associates.
> This programming book is source-code intensive with few illustrations. It includes lots and lots of well-documented Java source code.

The Companion CD-ROM

The companion CD-ROM includes:

- Complete Java source code for this book, ready-to-use in your own apps:
  - Runnable demos (console apps and GUIs)
  - Complete HTML documentation for the software, source code, and demos

- Together/J Whiteboard Edition, the first pure-Java UML modeler that delivers simultaneous round-trip engineering, a product that will help you get the most out of this book.

- Java design strategies in HTML

How to Get Updates

We'll post the most recent versions of the CD-ROM goodies at Object International's web site (www.oi.com). Check there for updates.

While visiting at that site, consider subscribing to the free newsletters and discussion groups—tools that can help you get the most out of this book.

Feedback, Hands-on Workshops, and Mentoring

Please feel free to send in feedback; it is much appreciated. In addition, if you are interested in custom-in-house workshops or mentoring, please visit our web sites for more information.

Peter Coad
President
Object International, Inc.
coad@oi.com   www.oi.com

Mark Mayfield
Senior Object-Model Architect
Net Explorer, Inc.
mayfield@netexplorer.com   www.netexplorer.com

Chapter 1

Design by Example

This chapter teaches design by example. Its sections are short and to the point—enough to establish notation processes, and two good examples—yet no longer than needed to set the stage for the four core chapters that follow.

In this chapter, you'll walk through two major examples, following these five major design activities:

- Identify purpose and features
- Select classes
- Sketch a user interface (UI)
- Work out dynamics with scenarios
- Build a class diagram

If you already practice object-oriented design, you might want to just scan this first chapter and then proceed to the Java-inspired chapters:

- Design with composition, rather than inheritance
- Design with interfaces

- Design with threads

- Design with notification

Let's begin.

1.1   Five Major Activities

The design approach you are about to experience consists of five major activities.

Please note that these are *activities*, not *steps*. If it weren't so impractical, one could place all five sections in parallel columns, jumping back and forth from one section to the next to illustrate the interdependent nature of these activities.

In practice, you'll gain a lot of synergy by working back and forth between these activities. Each activity will help you discover new content for the other activities.

Here's how the activites work together.

The *Identify Purpose and Features* activity will help you discover classes, understand UI needs, identify which scenarios are the ones to pay attention to, and grapple with what to include or not include within a class diagram. Notice how this one activity touches all of the others.

The *Select Classes* activity will help you challenge the breadth of purpose and features, establish UI content, and provide the building blocks for scenario views and a class diagram.

The *Sketch a UI* activity will help you discover new purpose and features, find additional classes, identify some of the most significant scenarios, and work out the UI influences within a class diagram.

The *Work Out Dynamics with Scenarios* activity will help you discover variations on purpose and features, find additional classes, add detail (e.g., action buttons) to the UI sketches, and add substance—specifically, "must have" methods—to a class diagram.

And yes, the *Build a Class Diagram* activity will help you discover additional purpose and features, apply patterns, add more classes and associations, refine the UI design, and discover new scenarios.

Apply these strategies synergistically, rather than sequentially. That's the way to get the most from them.

1.2 Example, Example, Example

The best way to teach is by example.

> *Example* is the school of mankind, and they will learn at no other.
> —Edmund Burke

> *Example* is not the main thing in influencing others, it is the only thing.
> —Albert Schweitzer

> *Example* isn't another way to teach, it is the only way to teach.
> —Albert Einstein

This book teaches by example, pointing out strategies and other important lessons along the way.

Two examples are woven throughout the very fabric of this book: a business example and a real-time example.

If you are a business app developer, study both examples. Carefully consider the business example. Then read the real-time example to gain added insights on concurrency and notification.

If you are a real-time system developer, study both examples. Read the business example first; that is where you'll find detailed "how to" strategies and discussions. Then study the real-time example, gaining additional insights into real-time issues along the way.

1.3   Charlie's Charters

The business example that runs throughout this book is called "Charlie's Charters" (Figure 1-1).

Charlie's Charters is a small regional carrier with small-aircraft service to nearby destinations. Charlie's Charters needs an application for scheduling flights and making reservations.

1.3.1   Identify the Purpose and Features

The first activity is identifying purpose and features.

1.3.1.1   Identify the Purpose

Begin by identifying the purpose of the system. What's this new application all about—its essence, its critical success factor, its unique selling proposition?

Identify the Purpose Strategy: *State the purpose of the system in 25 words or less.*

You could talk things over with the manager of Charlie's Charters and establish this purpose: to describe flights, to schedule flights, and to make reservations.

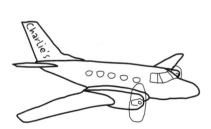

Figure 1-1.   Charlie's Charters.

By the way, some figures in this book have a "hand drawn" look to them, to engage more visually-oriented readers. This "look and feel" is intentional (although it took professional artists to take our rough sketches and transform them into something both casual and legible!). We hope that you'll enjoy the overall effect.

Sometimes you might have a hard time coming up with a concise system purpose statement. When that happens, shift gears and develop a features list first; then prioritize those features and incorporate the most important ones into an official-sounding system purpose statement.

1.3.1.2 Identify the Features

The next thing to do is to identify the features for this system.

Developers can get really (really) carried away, identifying feature after feature after feature.

How can you get to a meaningful features list?

Look for features that produce a desired outcome. The best features satisfy a "want" for the consumer who will be served by the system or a "want" for whomever is paying for the system.

Your customer will vote with his wallet. You need to deliver features that satisfy the "wants" of those two audiences. Adding extra bells and whistles, features that don't satisfy a "want," waste time, budget, talent, *and* profits.

Identify the Features Strategy: *List the features for setting up, conducting the business, and assessing business results.*

Apply this strategy to the Charlie's Charters application.

Setting up

1. Enter (add, change, delete) airports.

2. Enter flight descriptions.

3. Enter scheduled flights.

Conducting the business

4. Enter passengers.

5. Enter a reservation.

Assessing business results

6. Does a scheduled flight have any room left? (Assess this
   whenever you are getting ready to add reservation.)

You've defined system purpose and identified key features—a good
start.

Over time, you'll discover additional features and add them to your
list. And that's fine. Over time, you'll gain a better understanding
about what the customer really wants. This is not feature creep!
Yes, add features to your features list at any time. Yet until you com-
mit to doing them, until you add a milestone for that feature in the
project schedule, those newer features, are just proposed not com-
mitted-to features—a big difference.

Over time, you might need to update the overall purpose statement, too.

Change is inevitable. Early software development methods fought
change ("the requirements are fixed and cannot be changed on this
project"—a fantasy no longer possible in today's fast-paced world).
Effective object-oriented design embraces continual change.

1.3.2   Select the Classes

The second activity is selecting classes.

1.3.2.1   Object, Class

An *object* is a person, place, or thing. It's a noun. In software, it's a
small piece of running software with its own values and its own behavior.

For example, a "scheduled flight" *object* could have its own value (date = July 26) and its own behavior ("add reservation").

A *class* is a description that applies to each of some number of similar objects. In software, a class is where you write application code, establishing

- the interface for each object in that class (its method signatures)
- the internals for each object in that class
    - what each object knows (its attributes)
    - who each object knows (its associations)
    - what each object does (its methods).

It might also describe

- the interface for the class itself
- the internals for the class itself
    - what the class itself knows (its class attributes)
    - what each class does (its class methods).

A class also describes

    - how this class relates to other classes, namely, its superclasses.

For example, a "scheduled flight" *class* might describe

- an attribute called "date"
- an association to a "flight description" (a catalog entry, containing standard details about that flight)
- a method called "has room" (so each scheduled flight object can respond to the inquiry, "Do you have room for another passenger on this flight?")

1.3.2.2 Select the Classes

Select some initial classes. Look at persons, places, and things (objects) and form classes.

Person, place, or thing? It's worth expanding that list to cover the kinds of objects that you'll find again and again when building object models. Here is the strategy:

Select the Classes Strategy: *Feature by feature, look for: role-player, role, transaction (moment or interval), place, container, or catalog-like description. For real-time systems, also look for data acquisition and control devices.*

Apply this strategy to the Charlie's Charters application (see Figures 1-2 and 1-3):

1. Enter (add, change, delete) airports.

   place: airport

2. Enter flight descriptions.

   catalog-like description: flight description (flight number, arrival time, departure time, and the like)

3. Enter scheduled flights.

   transaction (moment or interval): scheduled flight

   place: airport

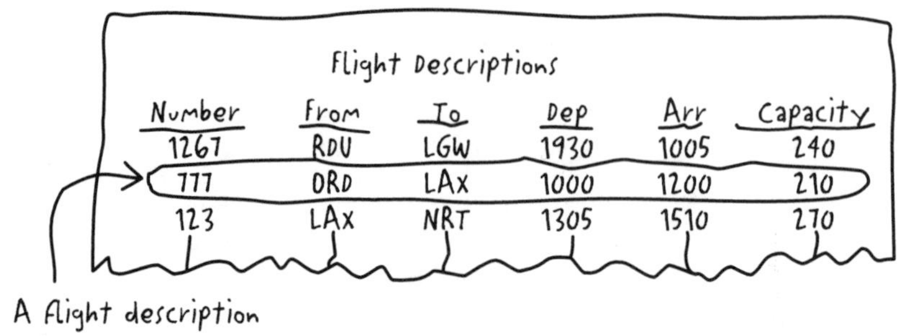

A flight description

Figure 1-2. Flight descriptions.

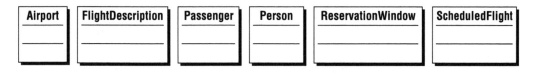

Figure 1-3.   Problem-domain classes for Charlie's Charters.

4. Enter a passenger.

> role-player: person
>
> role: passenger

5. Enter a reservation.

> role-player: person
>
> role: passenger
>
> catalog-like description: flight description
>
> transaction (moment or interval): reservation, scheduled flight

6. Does a scheduled flight have room? (needed when adding a reservation).

> transaction (moment or interval): scheduled flight

So far, so good. The classes are shown in Figure 1-3.

1.3.3   Sketch a UI

You've established system purpose and features and identified initial classes. The third activity is sketching out a user interface (UI), the windows and reports for delivering those features.

First, list the key ingredients, the content you need. Then sketch a mock-up.

1.3.3.1 List the Key Ingredients

UI Content Strategy: *Feature by feature, establish content: selections, lists, entry fields, display fields, actions, assessments.*

Apply this strategy to the Charlie's Charters application. For each feature, identify the supporting content you might require:

1. Enter airports.

    primary selection and list: airport; airport list

2. Enter flight descriptions.

    primary selection and list: flight description; flight-description list

    secondary selections and lists: from, to; from list, to list

    entry fields: flight number, departure time, arrival time

    actions: add a scheduled flight

3. Enter scheduled flights.

    primary selection and list: scheduled flight; scheduled-flight list

    secondary selection and list: flight description; flight-description list

    entry fields: date

    actions: has room?, add a reservation

4. Enter passengers.

    primary selection and list: passenger; passenger list

    entry fields: name, address, type (regular, gold, platinum)

    display fields: number

5. Enter a reservation.

    primary selection and list: passenger; passenger list

    secondary selection and list: flight description; flight-description list

    tertiary selection and list: scheduled flight; scheduled-flight list

    display fields: date and time made, expiration date and time

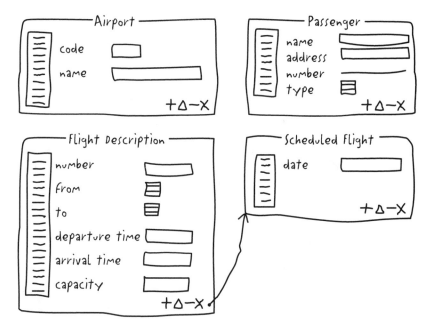

Figure 1-4.   Mock-ups for entering airports, flight descriptions, scheduled flights, and passengers.

1.3.3.2 Sketch a Mock-Up

With the content identified, you can quickly sketch the mock-ups of the UI.

Figure 1-4 is a sketch for entering airports, flight descriptions, scheduled flights, and passengers.

Figure 1-5 is a sketch for entering a reservation.

Based upon the UI sketches in Figures 1-4 and 1-5, you can add these initial UI classes to the object model (see Figure 1-6).

1.3.4   Work Out Dynamics with Scenarios

The fourth activity is working out dynamics with scenarios.

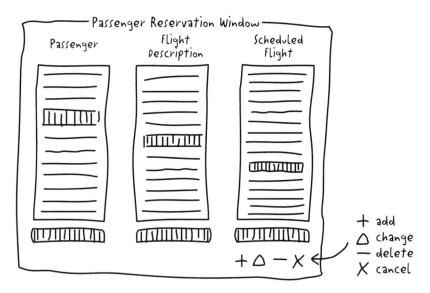

Figure 1-5. Mock-up for entering a reservation.

Figure 1-6. UI classes for Charlie's Charters.

1.3.4.1 Scenario Views for Setting Up

Work out the scenarios for setting up, to get everything ready for making reservations.

Normally, you won't work out most "setting up" scenarios because they are fairly simple. Once you've worked out several of them, the pattern is pretty clear and consistent:

- a UI object
- one or two problem-domain (PD) objects
- and some simple messaging:

- create and initialize an object
- possibly send it to another object, to connect the two to each other

1.3.4.1.1 Enter airports

The "enter airport" scenario describes the time-ordered sequence for building an airport window, followed by entering (adding, changing, or deleting) an airport.

A scenario is described as a sequence diagram portraying a time-ordered sequence of object interactions.

This scenario has four parts: build (the window), add an airport, change an airport, and delete an airport (Figure 1-7).

What about persistent storage? If we are working with an object DBMS, then the scenario is fine as it is (the object DBMS provides the needed infrastructure for loading, searching, and saving airport objects). If we are working with a relational DBMS, then the scenario view needs an additional class called AirportDM that is responsible for interacting with one or more tables in the database to provide the persistence mechanism. Working with relational databases is outside the scope of this book (if you are interested in this specific aspect of design, see [Coad97] and [CoadLetter]).

1.3.4.1.2 An aside: sequence-diagram notation

Here are some details about sequence diagram notation (see Figure 1-7).

In a sequence diagram, the boxes are objects.

The vertical dashed line descending from each object box is the lifeline, representing the time that object exists during the interaction sequence. Time moves vertically, from top to bottom.

The vertical rectangles are activation bars, showing when an object is participating in an interaction sequence, including the time its message recipients require.

The horizontal filled-arrowhead arrows are messages. Each message line represents both sending the message and (in due course)

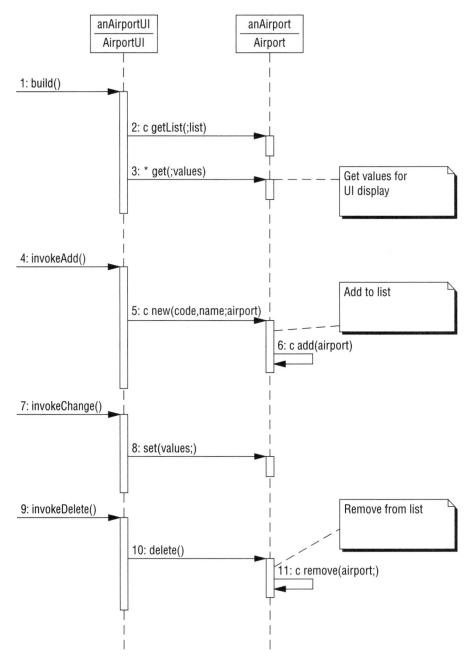

Figure 1-7. Build an airport window, then enter (add, change, and delete) an airport.

receiving a response. The label is the name of the message (corresponding to the method name it invokes). Arguments follow the convention: (inputs ; output). The message arrows go:

- From an object to another object (this is the norm)
- From an object back to itself (messaging itself)
- From an object to objects in a collection (shown by placing an asterisk before a message name)
- From an object to a class, for example, asking a class to create a new object (shown by placing a class marker, c, before a message name).

A precondition may appear before a message name (shown within square brackets).

Notes are notes. Use notes to highlight sections within a sequence diagram and to annotate sequences with keyword pairs such as IF/ENDIF, DO/ENDDO, and SYNC/ENDSYNC.

1.3.4.1.3   *Enter flight descriptions; enter passengers*
Enter flight descriptions. The class names are FlightDescriptionUI and FlightDescription. The "new" method creates an object and initializes it. That method's input parameters are number, from, to, departureTime, arrivalTime, capacity; the method returns a flight description.

Enter passengers. The class names are PassengerUI and Passenger. The parameters are: (name, address ; passenger).

Once you've done one of the "setting up" scenario views, you really don't get too excited about doing them again and again.

There is a variation on this theme, however, with a bit more to it. Take a look at it next.

1.3.4.1.4   *Enter scheduled flights*
When entering a scheduled flight, you select a corresponding flight description.

In fact, the same scenario shape applies whenever we need to enter an object (in this case, a scheduled flight) and select a related object (in this case, a flight description, standard catalog information for that flight).

The pattern is

- a UI object
- one or two PD objects
- and some simple messaging:

    create and initialize an object

    send it to another object, to connect the two to each other.

Figure 1-8 illustrates this kind of "setting up" scenario.

You cannot document every scenario for an application. Instead, focus on the scenarios that will give the most added value, the most insights. Where do you find them? Read on.

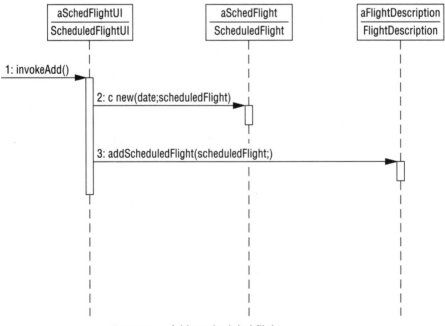

Figure 1-8.   Add a scheduled flight.

1.3.4.2 Scenarios for Conducting Business and Assessing Results

You'll spend much more of your time working with scenarios for the "conducting business" and "assessing results" features.

These scenarios demonstrate higher-value features, desired outcomes in which domain experts have more of a vested interest (and will work hard to get right).

These scenarios help you discover additional classes and methods, improving overall results.

High-Value Scenarios Strategy: *Build scenarios that will exercise each "conducting business" and "assessing results" feature.*

1.3.4.2.1 Enter a reservation
Continue working out the Charlie's Charters example, this time for entering a reservation (see Figure 1-9):

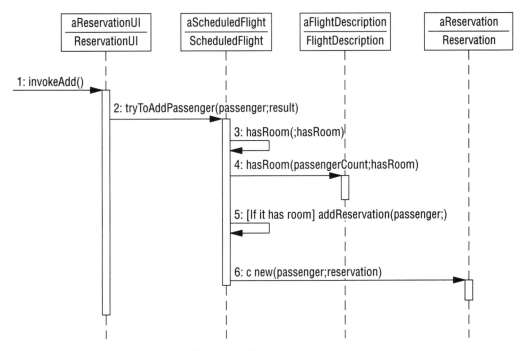

Figure 1-9.   Add a reservation.

Enter a reservation.

Select a passenger.

Select a flight description.

Select a scheduled flight.

Invoke "add reservation."

If the scheduled flight is not full, add a reservation.

Action Sentence Strategy: *Describe the action in a complete sentence. Put the action in the object (person, place, or thing) that has the "what I know" and "who I know" to get the job done.*

Charlie's Charters example:

Complete sentence: Is the scheduled flight full?

Put the action in the object: scheduled flight.

What happens if users attempt to make more than one reservation at a time? Could you get into trouble here, overbooking without knowing it? Chapter 4 explores this in detail.

1.3.5   Build a Class Diagram

At this point, you've already got a lot of content for a class diagram:

- PD classes

- UI classes

- Methods

- And some hints at associations (unless someone passes the receiver as a parameter, a sender needs an association to maintain to whom to send a message).

Indeed, it's good to build a class diagram in parallel with working out scenarios. There is lot of synergy between a class diagram and its scenario views. These two kinds of diagrams are the must-have ingredients of an effective object model.

Here's the strategy:

Build a Class Diagram Strategy:

Start with scenario classes and methods.

Add attributes

Add associations—message paths for methods.

Add associations—look-up paths for the UI.

1.3.5.1 Class Diagram Model—PD Component

Build a class diagram for the PD component (see Figure 1-10):

- Class: Person

    attributes: name, address

    association: passenger

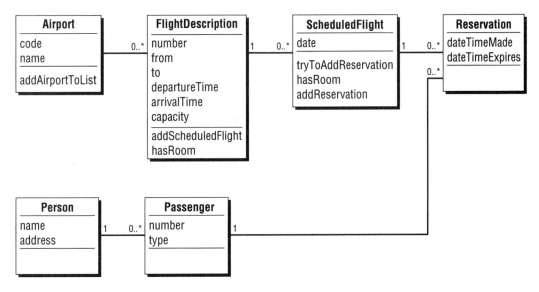

Figure 1-10. A class diagram—PD component.

- Class: Passenger

    attributes: number, type (regular, gold, platinum)

    associations (look-up paths): person, scheduled flight

- Class: Reservation

    attributes: date and time made, expiration date and time

    associations (look-up paths): passenger, scheduled flight

- Class: Scheduled Flight

    instance methods: try to add passenger, has room, add passenger

    attribute: date

    associations (look-up paths): reservation, flight description

    association (message path): flight description

- Class: Flight Description

    instance methods: add scheduled flight, has room

    attributes: flight number, from, to, departure time, arrival time

    associations (look-up paths): scheduled flight, airport

- Class: Airport

    attributes: (three-letter) code, description

    association (look-up path): flight description

Note that the methods in Figure 1-10 are exactly those methods we've added by working out dynamics with scenarios.

Class diagrams usually do not include frequently occurring methods (for example, getters and setters, constructors, adds and removes, and deletes. Why? It brings greater emphasis to the other methods in the diagram. Note that you will see such methods, placed within a specific context within a scenario.

1.3.5.2 Class-Diagram Notation

The following sections present some notes on class-diagram notation.*

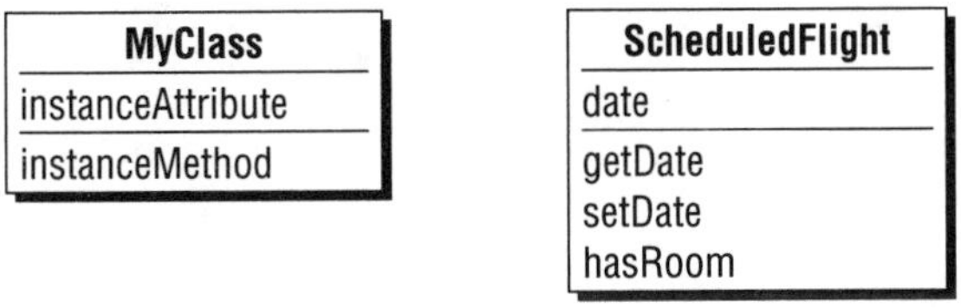

MyClass
instanceAttribute
instanceMethod

ScheduledFlight
date
getDate
setDate
hasRoom

Figure 1-11.   Two classes.

1.3.5.2.1   *Class*

Take a closer look at the classes presented in Figure 1-11.

A rectangle represents a class with the potential for some number of objects in that class.

By convention, class names begin with a capital letter, for example, the ScheduledFlight class. Object names begin with a lowercase letter, for example, a scheduledFlight object is an object of the class ScheduledFlight.

The class symbol is divided into three sections: class name, attributes, and methods.*

In these examples:

Each object in the class MyClass

- holds its own value for instanceAttribute, and
- carries out the instanceMethod.

Each object in the class ScheduledFlight will

- hold its own value for date,
- carry out the accessor methods (getDate, setDate), and
- carry out the hasRoom method.

---

*What Java calls a method, UML calls an operation. This book uses the Java name for this concept.

Now, you can express a design graphically (in a class diagram) or textually (in Java code itself). You've seen ScheduledFlight graphically. What does it look like in Java? It looks like this:*

```
public class ScheduledFlight {
✂
    // attributes / private
    private Date date;

    // methods / public / accessors for attribute values
    public Date getDate() { return this.date; }
    public void setDate(Date aDate) { this.date = aDate; }

    // methods / public / conduct business
    public boolean hasRoom() {
        /* code goes in here */ }
✂
}
```

The little scissors (✂) symbols designate Java *snippets*, small and to-the-point excerpts of Java code, illustrating key concepts along the way. (These Java snippets can be found on the companion CD.)

1.3.5.2.2   Expanded "class with objects" symbol

Now consider an expanded version of the two examples (see Figure 1-12).

A class name in italics indicates that the class is an abstract class. An abstract class is a class without any possibility of having corresponding objects.

The class symbol has some added information. The underlined attributes and methods are class members, *not* instance members.

---

*Style note: We prefer to limit access to all attributes, including class attributes; we make them private and use accessors to get and set values. This convention is consistent, easy to follow, and hard to foul up.

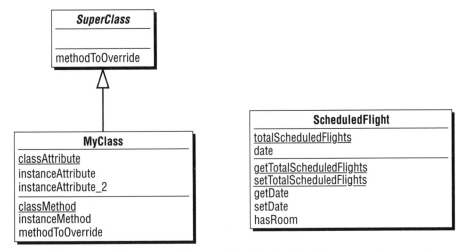

Figure 1-12. Two expanded examples showing inheritance and class members.

Class attributes have a value that applies across the collection of all of the objects in a class; if all flight descriptions had to abide by a "never to exceed" capacity, then we would need a class attribute.

Instance attributes are those attributes for which each object in a class can have its own values.

Class methods apply across the collection of all of the objects in a class; methods like new (create and initialize a new object and add it to the collection of all of the objects in that class), getList, and "find the object that matches this description" are class methods. Class methods can only access class attributes (no "this" reference).

Instance methods are those methods that each object in the class can do on its own.

In these examples:

Each object in the class Class:

- holds its own value for instanceAttribute, and

- carries out the instanceMethod.

- implements methodToOverride

In addition, the class MyClass:

- holds its own value for classAttribute, and
- carries out the classMethod.

Each object in the class ScheduledFlight will:

- hold its own value for date,
- carry out the accessor methods (getDate, setDate), and
- carry out the hasRoom method.

In addition, the class ScheduledFlight will:

- hold its own value for totalScheduledFlights, and
- carry out getTotalScheduledFlights and setTotalScheduled-Flights methods

    (the "set" should be private, something that only the class itself can invoke).

Once again, you can express the design graphically (in a class diagram) or textually (in Java code itself).

How can you express ScheduledFlight's class attribute and class methods in Java? Take a look:

```
public class ScheduledFlight {
✂
    // class attributes / private
    private static int totalScheduledFlights;

    // class methods / public / accessors for class attribute values
    public static int getTotalScheduledFlights() { return totalScheduledFlights; }
    // class methods / private / accessors for class attribute values
    private static void setTotalScheduledFlights(int total) {
        totalScheduledFlights = total; }
✂
}
```

1.3.5.3 Association

An association is a mapping between an object in one class with some number of objects in another class. In addition, associations define some of the likely look-up paths and message paths. Associations establish the "who I know" aspect of an object's responsibilities.

If an association carries the added meaning of whole-part (assembly-part, container-contents, or group-member), it is called and aggregation. An aggregation gets a little diamond at the beginning of the line, next to the "whole."

Associations have cardinalities. Cardinalities are text tags that express, "As an object in a class at one end of a link, how many objects at the other end of the link may I (or must I) hold?" The cardinality at the other end of the link answers that question.

The most common cardinalities are:

0 . . 1	zero to one
1	one
0 . . *	zero to many
1 . . *	one to many
[description] cardinality	qualified cardinality

Again, you can express a design graphically (in a class diagram) or textually (in Java code itself).

First, express it graphically: Consider the association between scheduled flight and reservation (see Figure 1-13).

How do you read this? Start at one end: "A scheduled-flight object has . . ." And then jump across to the other end for the cardinality and associated class: "A scheduled-flight object holds some number of reservation objects."

Reading the other direction: "A reservation knows a scheduled-flight object."

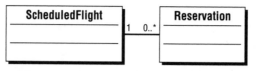

Figure 1-13. The association between ScheduledFlight and Reservation.

Second, express it textually: Implement the association between a scheduled flight and its reservations in Java.

```
public class ScheduledFlight {

    // attributes / private / associations
    private Vector reservations = new Vector();

    // methods / public / accessors for association values
    public void addReservation(Reservation aReservation) {
        this.reservations.addElement(aReservation); }
    public void removeReservation(Reservation aReservation) {
        this.reservations.removeElement(aReservation); }

    // methods / public / get enumeration of reservations vector
    public Enumeration getReservationList() {
        return this.reservations.elements(); }

    // methods / protected / accessor for association vector
    protected Vector getReservations() {
        return this.reservations; }

}
```

Code note: This code initializes the reservations variable as a Vector object, rather than null (the default). Alternatively it could initialize the variable with a constructor.

Code note: This code limits visibility of getReservations to ScheduledFlight's subclasses. Others gain access through an Enumeration.

```
public class Reservation {

    // attribute / private / association
    private ScheduledFlight scheduledFlight;
```

```
// methods / public / accessors for association values
public void addScheduledFlight(ScheduledFlight aScheduledFlight) {
        this.scheduledFlight = aScheduledFlight; }
public ScheduledFlight getScheduledFlight() { return this.scheduledFlight; }
public void removeScheduledFlight() { this.scheduledFlight = null; }
```
✄
```
}
```

1.3.5.4 Class Diagram—UI Component

Next, build a class diagram for the classes for the UI component, by applying the same "Build a class diagram" strategy. Figure 1-14 shows the result.

Note that each window class has attribute pairs: a list of objects and a selected one (or selected ones, in contexts that warrant multiple selections).

Take a closer look at these attributes. A list of objects? A selected object? Those attributes sound like associations in disguise. And they are—associations shown in text. That's the best way to show an association from UI objects to PD objects. Why? Well, UI objects show a view of the PD objects, and consequently tend to be very interconnected with some number of PD objects. Using text makes this interconnection easier to understand (a picture is worth a thousand words; though here a few words greatly simplifies the picture).

How do these UI objects get the values they need? For the *list attribute:* A UI object sends a message to a PD class, asking for a list

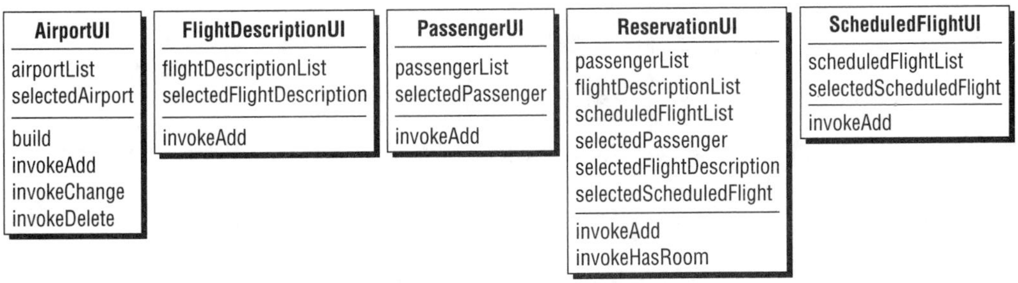

AirportUI	FlightDescriptionUI	PassengerUI	ReservationUI	ScheduledFlightUI
airportList selectedAirport	flightDescriptionList selectedFlightDescription	passengerList selectedPassenger	passengerList flightDescriptionList scheduledFlightList selectedPassenger selectedFlightDescription selectedScheduledFlight	scheduledFlightList selectedScheduledFlight
build invokeAdd invokeChange invokeDelete	invokeAdd	invokeAdd	invokeAdd invokeHasRoom	invokeAdd

Figure 1-14. A class diagram—UI component.

of its objects. Then the UI object sends messages to each object in that list, to get the values it needs for display. For the *selection attribute:* Someone makes a selection, and then the UI object knows the selected object.

Most methods in these UI classes begin with "invoke," meaning, someone takes a UI action, and that invokes a corresponding set of actions.

1.3.5.5 Class Diagram for Charlie's Charters

At this point, the overall class diagram for Charlie's Charters looks like Figure 1-15.

You'll see more of Charlie's Charters in the chapters ahead.

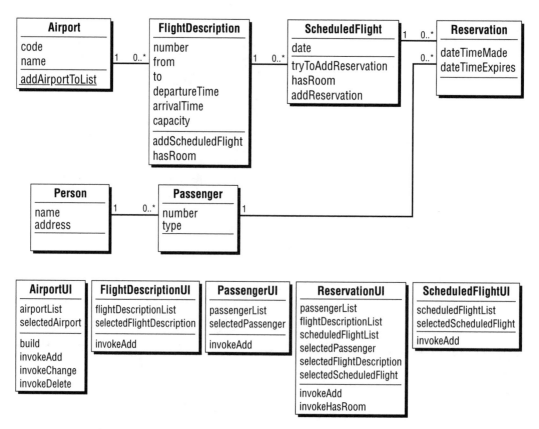

Figure 1-15. A class diagram for Charlie's Charters.

1.4 Zoe's Zones

A real-time example?

Please kindly note that by including a real-time example, we are not at all suggesting that we build *time-critical* real-time applications with Java—no way (not yet, anyway).

This book is about Java-inspired design, not about Java programming. The lessons learned here are applicable to design with other languages, too (including C++, Smalltalk, Object Pascal, Eiffel, and Ada).

We include a real-time example here so we can (1) work with an example that engineers can more easily relate to, and (2) illustrate certain concurrency issues along the way.

The real-time example that runs throughout this book is called "Zoe's Zones."

Zoe develops and delivers monitoring systems consisting of zones and sensors and a centralized monitoring station (see Figure 1-16).

A zone is a collection of sensors, typically located within a room, floor, assembly line, building, or facility.

A sensor is a data acquisition device that measures a given system variable and provides an output signal for other devices/systems to read. For example, different types of sensors might detect temperature, pressure, smoke level, or motion.

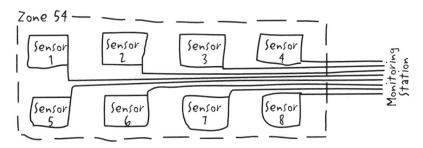

Figure 1-16.   Zoe's Zones.

This example is streamlined, offering just a few comments along the way. It is a different problem domain, yet the same activities apply:

- Identify purpose and features
- Select classes
- Sketch a UI
- Work out dynamics with scenarios
- Build a class diagram

1.4.1   Identify the Purpose and Features

The first activity is identifying purpose and features.

1.4.1.1 Identify the System Purpose

Begin by identifying the purpose of the system.

Purpose: to monitor and track problem reports from sensors, grouped into zones.

1.4.1.2 Identify the Features

Follow up by identifying the features of the system:

Setting up

1. Enter sensors.
2. Enter zones.

Conducting the business

3. Activate zones and sensors.
4. Record problem intervals.

Assessing business results

5. Assess sensor reliability.

1.4.2   Selecting Classes

The second activity is selecting classes (see Figure 1-17):

Setting up

1. Enter sensors

    data-acquisition device: sensor

2. Enter zones

    place, container: zone

Conducting the business

3. Activate zones and sensors

    data-acquisition device: sensor

    place, container: zone

4. Record problem intervals

    transaction (moment or interval): problem interval

Assessing business results

5. View problem intervals

    transaction (moment or interval): problem interval

6. Assess sensor reliability

    data-acquisition device: sensor

    transaction (moment or interval): problem interval

ProblemInterval	Sensor	Zone

Figure 1-17.   Problem-domain classes for Zoe's Zones.

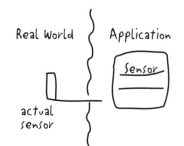

Figure 1-18. An actual sensor vs. an abstraction of an application's responsibilities for interacting with an actual sensor.

The symbols in Figure 1-17 represent classes for the software application that will serve the monitoring station.

It is important to note that the objects in these classes are *abstractions*, not the real things.

A problem-interval object abstracts an interval of time between problem detection and problem correction. It is not an interval of absolute (or wall clock) time; instead, it is an abstraction of what the application knows and does about that interval of time.

A zone object abstracts a zone of sensors. It is not an actual zone; instead, it is an abstraction of what the application knows and does about each zone.

Similarly, a sensor object abstracts a sensor. It is not an actual sensor; instead, it is an abstraction, a mere proxy, representing what the application knows and does to interact with an actual, physical sensor (see Figure 1-18).

Even though you might know a great deal about a physical object, do your best to model only just what you need to get the job done—no more, no less.

1.4.3   Sketch a UI

The third activity is sketching out a UI.

1.4.3.1 List the Key Ingredients

Begin by listing the key ingredients, the required information you need for the UI:

1. Enter sensors

   primary selection and list: sensor, sensor list

   entry fields: number, interval

   actions: activate, assess reliability

2. Enter zones

   primary selection and list: zone, zone list

   secondary selection and list: sensor, sensor list

   entry fields:

     for zone: number, threshold

     for each sensor in the zone: number

   actions: activate, accept report (from a sensor)

3. View problem intervals

   list: problem interval list

1.4.3.2 Sketch It Out

With the content identified, now sketch a UI for entering sensors and zones (see Figure 1-19).

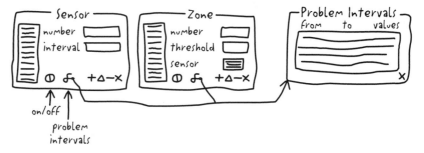

Figure 1-19. Mock-ups for entering sensor, entering zones, and looking at problem intervals.

Figure 1-20.   UI classes for Zoe's Zones.

Put the corresponding UI classes into a class diagram (see Figure 1-20).

1.4.4   Work Out Dynamics with Scenarios

The fourth activity is working out dynamics with scenarios.

1.4.4.1   Scenarios for Setting Up

Begin by working out the scenarios for setting up, getting everything ready to go for monitoring sensors within zones.

1.4.4.1.1   *Enter sensors*
Start out with a simple one, the "add a sensor" scenario (see Figure 1-21).

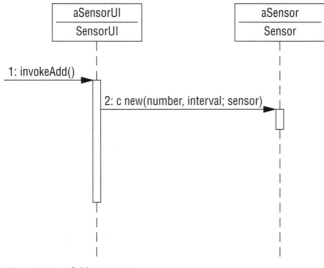

Figure 1-21.   Add a sensor.

1.4.4.1.2 Enter zones

"An enter zones" scenario follows the same basic pattern and so it is not shown here. The class names change to "ZoneUI" and "Zone." The parameters are: (number, threshold ; zone).

1.4.4.2 Scenarios for Conducting Business and Assessing Results

Apply the "high-value scenarios" strategy to the Zoe's Zones application.

1. Activate a zone and its sensors. Try the "action sentence" strategy here. You could ask a zone object to activate itself. Then it could tell each of its sensors to activate itself (see Figure 1-22).

2. Record problem intervals (see Figure 1-23).

3. View problem intervals (see Figure 1-24).

4. Assess sensor reliability (see Figure 1-25).

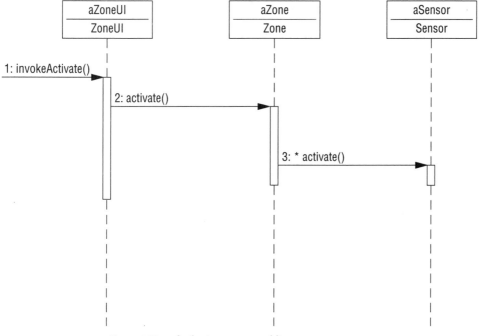

Figure 1-22. Activate a zone and its sensors.

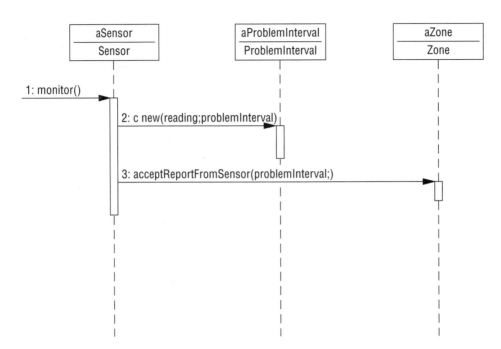

Figure 1-23. Record problem intervals.

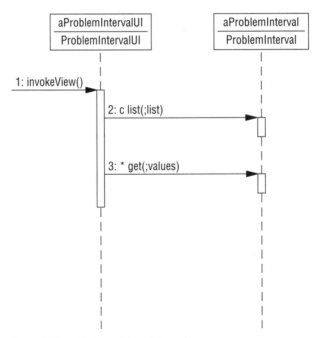

Figure 1-24. View problem intervals.

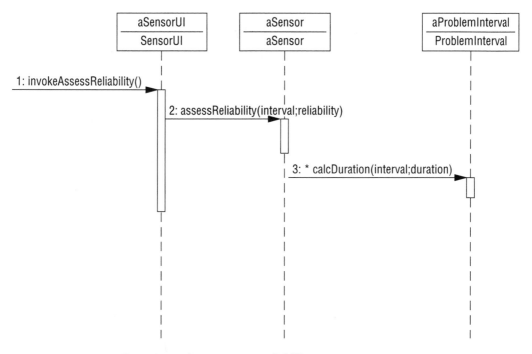

Figure 1-25.   Assess sensor reliability.

1.4.5   Build a Class Diagram

The fifth activity is building a class diagram.

1.4.5.1 Class Diagram—PD Component

At this point, you've already got a lot of content for a class diagram. Apply the "build a class diagram" strategy again:

- Sensor

  attribute: number, legal range, operational state

  (usually, a device object needs to keep track of its own operational state)

- association (look-up path): problem interval

  (if you needed the query: given a sensor, tell me its zone—then you'd need a look-up path from sensor to zone, too)

- association (message path): zone, problem interval

  actions: activate, monitor (on-going behavior), assess reliability

- Zone

    attribute: number, threshold

    association (look-up path): sensor, problem interval

    association (message path): sensor, problem interval

    actions: activate, monitor (on-going behavior), accept report (from a sensor)

- Problem interval

    attribute: date and time detected, worst value, date and time corrected

    association (look-up path): sensor or zone

    action: calculate duration

The result? See Figure 1-26.

1.4.5.2 "Kinds of"—Some Notes

Should you consider two different *kinds of* problem intervals?

- Sensor problem interval

    attribute: date and time detected, value, date and time corrected

    association: sensor

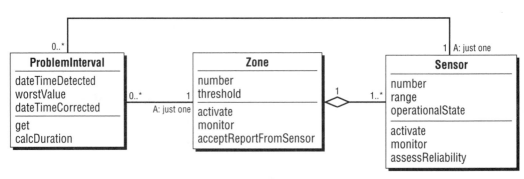

Figure 1-26. Object model—PD component.

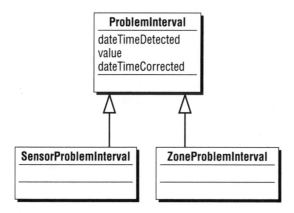

Figure 1-27. Kinds of problem reports.

- Zone problem interval

    attribute: date and time detected, value, date and time corrected

    association: zone

The two kinds of problem intervals are very similar. You could organize them with generalization-specialization, as shown in Figure 1-27.

However, the only difference between the two specialization classes is the kind of thing it is: sensor or zone.

Using specialization classes to describe what is nothing more than an enumeration of values is definitely overkill.

Hence, for now at least, a simple problem-interval class, as shown earlier in Figure 1-26, will do the trick:

- Problem interval

    attribute: date and time detected, value, date and time corrected

    association: either sensor or zone, but not both.

1.4.5.3 Associations—Some Notes

The association between a problem report and its sensor or zone tells us what kind of problem report it is. So you don't need an explicit "type" attribute. (If and when you need to know, you can ask the connecting object whether it is an instance of sensor or an instance of zone.)

Note the "A: just one" label in Figure 1-26. These markings indicate that each problem-interval object has an association to a sensor or to a zone, not both.

Here's what the association looks like in Java:

```
public class ProblemInterval {
✂
    // attribute / private / association
    private Object reporter;

    // methods / public / accessors for association values
    public void addReporter(Object aReporter) {
        this.reporter = aReporter; }
    public Object getReporter() { return this.reporter; }
    public void removeReporter() { this.reporter = null; }
✂
}
```

Code notes: The reporter attribute holds a Zone or a Sensor. The type of object held in this connection can be determined by asking the object for its class.

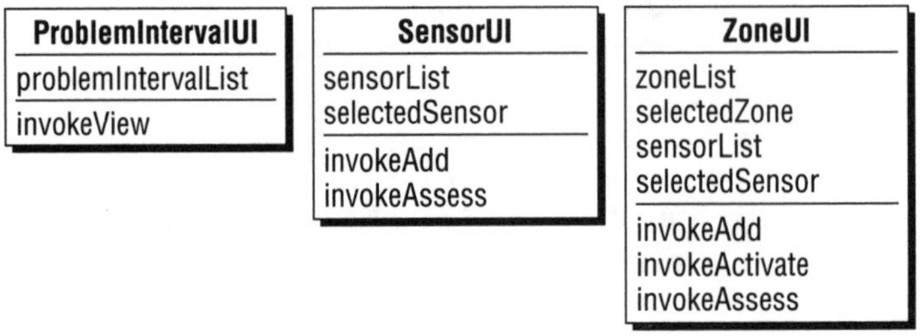

ProblemIntervalUI	SensorUI	ZoneUI
problemIntervalList	sensorList	zoneList
invokeView	selectedSensor	selectedZone
	invokeAdd	sensorList
	invokeAssess	selectedSensor
		invokeAdd
		invokeActivate
		invokeAssess

Figure 1-28.   Class Diagram—UI component.

1.4.5.4 Class Diagram—UI Component

Based on the UI sketches, add classes to the UI component (see Figure 1-28).

That's it for now. You'll see more of Zoe's Zones in the chapters ahead.

1.5   Summary

In this chapter, you've worked with scenarios and class diagrams for a business application (Charlie's Charters) and a real-time system (Zoe's Zones).

Along the way, you've learned and applied sequence-diagram notation (showing a time-ordered sequence of object interactions) and class-diagram notation (showing the responsibilities of each class of objects and each object within that class).

You've worked with these specific strategies for designing better apps:

Identify the Purpose Strategy: State the purpose of the system in 25 words or less.

Identify the Features Strategy: List the features for setting up, conducting the business, and assessing business results.

Select the Classes Strategy: Feature by feature, look for: role-player, role, transaction (moment or interval), place, container, or catalog-like description. For real-time systems, also look for data acquisition and control devices.

UI Content Strategy: Feature by feature, establish content: selections, lists, entry fields, display fields, actions, assessments.

High-Value Scenarios Strategy: Build scenarios that will exercise each "conducting business" and "assessing results" feature.

Action Sentence Strategy: *Describe the action in a complete sentence. Put the action in the object (person, place, or thing) that has the "what I know" and "who I know" to get the job done.*

Build a Class-Diagram Strategy:

Start with scenario classes and methods.

Add attributes

Add associations—message paths for methods.

Add associations—look-up paths for the UI.

Onward—to the core chapters of Java Design!

Chapter 2

Design with Composition, Rather than Inheritance

Composition and inheritance are both mechanisms for extending a design.

A number of years ago (and perhaps still, in the minds of some designers), inheritance was the only tool for extending responsibilities, and designers used it *everywhere*.

But extending responsibilities with inheritance is applicable only in very specific contexts. In nearly every case, extending the responsibilities with interfaces or with composition is more appropriate.

Use *composition* to extend responsibilities by delegating work to other more appropriate objects.

Use *inheritance* to extend attributes and methods. Note, however, with inheritance, encapsulation is inherently weak within a class hierarchy, so it's a good idea to use this mechanism only when certain criteria are met.

2.1   Composition

Composition extends the responsibilities of an object by delegating work to additional objects.

Composition is *the* major mechanism for extending the responsibilities of an object. Nearly every object in an object model is composed of, knows of, or works with other objects (composition).

2.1.1   Composition: An Example

Here's the composition strategy.

Composition Strategy: *Use Composition to extend responsibilities by delegating work to other objects.*

Figure 2-1 shows an example from Charlie's Charters. In this case, passenger objects need to have the ability to hold reservations.

This is an example of composition: a passenger object is a composition of some number of reservation objects.

How about in the other direction? A reservation object must have a single connection back to a passenger object.

Just a single connection? That's okay. It's still a composition.*

---

*A special kind of composition is called containment. It describes a composition in which the objects inside are hidden from all outsiders; access to what is inside is strictly limited to access via the container object. Most composition is *not* containment. A passenger object, with regard to its reservation objects, is composition, but not containment. A passenger object, with regard to its internal low-level objects such as strings, is often a container—a special kind of composition.

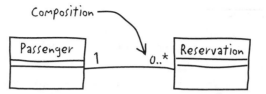

Figure 2-1.   A passenger object is able to holds some number of reservation objects.

2.2   Inheritance

Inheritance is a mechanism for extending the responsibilities defined in a class, meaning, to take the defined attributes, associations, and methods of a superclass and *add to them* in some way.

You can define basic common attributes, associations, and methods in a superclass (generalization class). Then you can add to them in one or more subclasses (specialization classes).

A subclass inherits everything that is defined in its superclass, accepting the superclass' definitions as its own.

2.2.1   Inheritance vs. Interfaces

Inheritance extends the *implementation of a method*, not just its interface.

An interface establishes *useful sets of method signatures*, without implying an implementation of a method.

In Java, inheritance and polymorphism (the ability to hide different implementations behind a common interface) are expressed distinctly with different syntax.

In C++, both concepts are expressed with a single syntax blurring the distinction between these very different mechanisms.

2.2.2   Inheritance: An Example

Inheritance is great for showing a class that is always a special variant of its "parent" class. Within a PD component of a class diagram, inheritance most often occurs in three situations (see Figure 2-2).

For example, consider transactions (notable moments or intervals of time). If the scope were to expand a bit at Charlie's Charters, you might discover that you need an object model like the one depicted in Figure 2-3.

A reservation is a special kind of transaction. A purchase is a special kind of transaction. So far, so good.

2.2.3   Inheritance: Benefits

Inheritance explicitly captures commonality, taking a class definition (what's the same: attributes, method signatures, and methods)

Figure 2-2.   The three most likely kinds of PD inheritance.

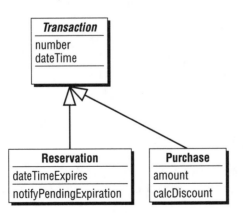

Figure 2-3.   Kinds of transactions.

and extending it with a new class definition (what's different: attributes, method signatures, and methods).

Inheritance is explicitly shown in a class diagram and in source code—something very nice indeed; so it's good to use, when it's appropriate to do so.

So, what are the risks?

2.2.4 Inheritance: Risks

Yes, inheritance does have its risks. Let's take a closer look at them.

2.2.4.1 Weak Encapsulation Within

Risk #1 Inheritance connotes strong encapsulation with other classes, but weak encapsulation between a superclass and its subclasses.

The classes within a class hierarchy, with respect to each other, violate the spirit of encapsulation, a fundamental tenet of object-oriented design. Subclasses are not well shielded from the potential ripple effect of changes in superclasses.

If you change a superclass, you must check all of its subclasses to correct any rippling change effects (Figure 2-4). Here's why: If you

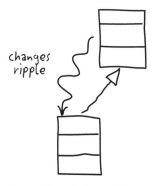

Figure 2-4. A change in a superclass ripples throughout its subclasses.

change the implementation of a class that is a superclass, then you have effectively changed the implementation of all its subclasses (testers, please take note).

Obviating risk #1   You can obviate this risk by designing a cohesive class hierarchy. Make sure the subclass is indeed a special kind of the superclass, not merely

- a factoring-out of common method implementations (a hard-to-understand, even harder to reuse hacker's trick), or

- a role played by the superclass (composition is a more flexible, more scalable way to model roles played).

Also, make sure that subclasses are indeed extensions. If you find the need to override or nullify inherited responsibilities, then you can

- introduce new superclasses (if you can), including one with exactly what you need to inherit (no more, no less), or

- define the class elsewhere. Then use composition to invoke whatever responsibilities you might need from the class hierarchy you shunned. (If you'd like to interact exactly like the objects in that hierarchy, just add an interface [see Chapter 3].)

2.2.4.2 Clumsy Accommodation of Objects that Change Subclasses

Risk #2   Inheritance connotes weak accommodation of objects that change subclasses over time.

For example, consider Person and its specializations, as shown in Figure 2-5. (No, you can't do multiple inheritance in Java, yet suppose for a moment that you could.)

What if you create an agent object, but later find out that you need an agent-passenger object? Consider the transition from an agent object to an agent-passenger object. Figure 2-6 illustrates what happens.

Every time an object in one subclass needs to change into an object in another class, you encounter the "transmute" problem: create an object in another class, copy values to the new object, then delete the old object.

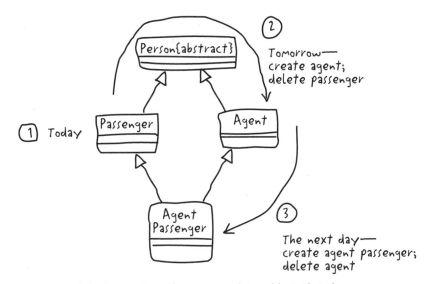

Figure 2-5. Inheritance clumsily accommodates objects that change subclasses (not an option in Java).

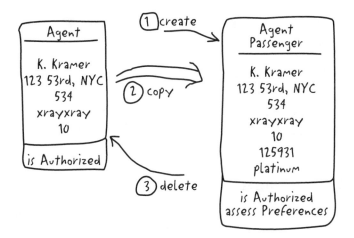

Figure 2-6. Create, copy, delete—"transmute."

When an object in a design transmutes, you might lose information. If the values are not needed in the new object, the old values go away.

Also, when an object transmutes, it loses all sense of history (even the question, "so how long have you been an agent?" is not easily answered, and requires additional classes to track such change over time). This makes change far more complex than it needs to be.

Obviating risk #2   Use composition of roles to obviate the risk. Composition is far better suited to continual change.

When an object needs additional role-specific responsibilities, add another role object (composition).

Adding a new role is easy. In fact, with kinds of roles, you could apply composition (a person and its roles) *and* inheritance (person roles, specializing into special kinds of roles). See Figure 2-7.

2.2.5   Inheritance: When to Use It

In bibliographic classification, developers of classification methods strive to find a way to classify publications so that

1. a subclass expresses "is a special kind of," not "is a role played by a"

2 an object, once classified, will forever remain an object in that class.

In software classification, one strives to find a way to classify objects (publications) so that

1. a subclass expresses "is a special kind of," not "is a role played by a"

2. an object, once classified, will forever remain an object in that class (it does not ever feel the need to transmute, to become an object in some other class).

In software classification, we add

3. a subclass extends, rather than overrides or nullifies, the responsibilities of its superclass

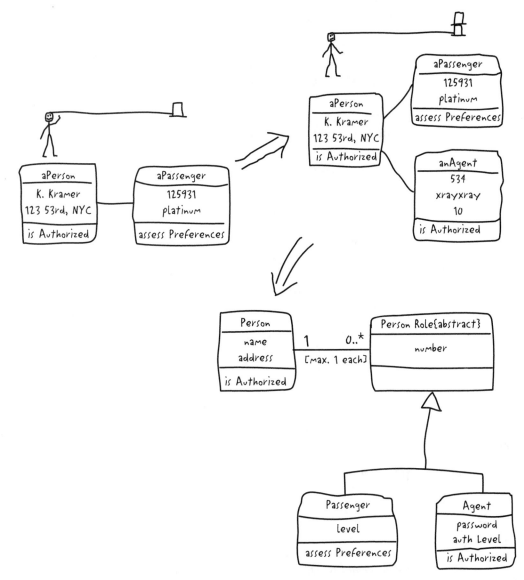

Figure 2-7. With composition, adding a new role is a breeze; if you have multiple kinds of roles, then inheritance can play along too.

4. a subclass does not extend the capabilities of what is merely a utility class (useful functionality you'd like to reuse)

5.   for PD classes, a subclass is a type of role played, transaction, or thing.

Here's how item 5 fits in. You can use inheritance in the PD component of an object model in three major ways:

- Role, specializing into special kinds of "participant" or "mission" roles

    - a role that a person plays:

        person role (passenger, clerk, head clerk, manager, owner)

    - a role that a facility or piece of equipment plays:

        aircraft mission (civilian mission, military mission)

- Transaction, specializing into special kinds of transactions (moments or intervals of time)

    - customer transaction (membership, reservation, payment, refund)

- Thing, specializing into special kinds of things

    - radar sensor (passive radar sensor, active radar sensor).

2.2.6   Inheritance: Checkpoints

The following strategy lists the five checkpoints for effective use of inheritance (see Figure 2-8).

When to Inherit Strategy: *Inheritance is used to extend attributes and methods; but encapsulation is weak within a class hierarchy, so use of this mechanism is limited. Use it when you can satisfy the following criteria:*

1. *"Is a special kind of," not "is a role played by a"*

2. *Never needs to transmute to be an object in some other class*

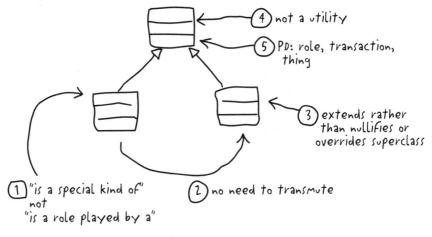

Figure 2-8. Inheritance criteria.

3. *Extends rather than overrides or nullifies superclass*

4. *Does not subclass what is merely a utility class (useful functionality you'd like to reuse)*

5. *Within PD: expresses special kinds of roles, transactions, or things*

2.3 Example: Composition (the Norm)

Consider a person and the roles he or she plays, the hats he or she wears: passenger and agent. Composition is the norm rather than the exception.

However, could you apply inheritance with person as a super-class, plus passenger, agent, and agent-passenger as subclasses? (See Figure 2-9.)

Well, in Java you can't do that. It's a single-inheritance language, and the agent-passenger class inherits from more than one class— multiple inheritance.

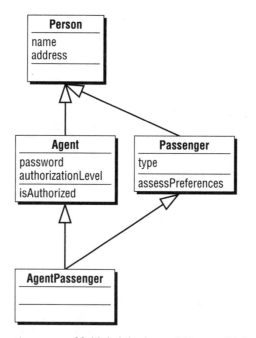

Figure 2-9. Multiple inheritance? Not a valid Java design.

Even if multiple inheritance were available, as it is in C++, is this an occasion to use inheritance, or would composition be better?

Apply the checkpoints strategy and check it out:

1. "Is a special kind of," not "is a role played by a"

    Fail. A passenger is not a kind of person; it's a role a person plays. An agent is not a kind of person; it's a role that a person plays.

2. Never needs to transmute to be an object in some other class

    Fail. It could change from passenger to agent to agent passenger, over time.

3. Extends rather than overrides or nullifies

    Pass. Okay here.

4. Does not subclass what is merely a utility class

    Pass. Okay here.

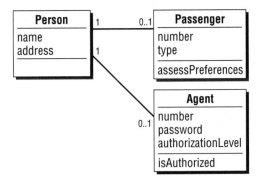

Figure 2-10. Person and two roles: passenger, and agent.

5. Within PD: Expresses special kinds of roles, transactions, or things

> Fail. This is not a kind of role, transaction, or thing.

Inheritance? No way. Composition applies here as is true in most cases of building better object models. It's the norm.

Take a look at Charlie's Charters. You could pick any association in the class diagram and find composition hard at work. Figure 2-10 provides an example (with a couple of methods, for good measure).

In Java, it looks like this:

```
public class Person {

    // attributes / private / associations
    private Passenger passenger;
    private Agent agent;

    // methods / public / accessors for association values
    public void addPassenger(Passenger aPassenger) {
        this.passenger = aPassenger; }
    public void removePassenger() { this.passenger = null; }
    public Passenger getPassenger() { return this.passenger; }
    public void addAgent(Agent anAgent) {
        this.agent = anAgent; }
```

```
        public void removeAgent() { this.agent = null; }
        public Agent getAgent() { return this.agent; }
✂
}
public class Passenger {
✂
        // attributes / private / associations
        private Person person;

        // methods / public / accessors for association values
        public Person getPerson() { return this.person; }

        // constructors
        // notice that there is no *default* constructor; a passenger must have
        // a corresponding person object.
        public Passenger(Person aPerson) {
            // implicit call to superclass constructor super();
            this.person = aPerson; }
✂
}
public class Agent {
✂
        // attributes / private / associations
        private Person person;

        // methods / public / accessors for association values
        public Person getPerson() { return this.person; }

        // constructors
        // note that there is no *default* constructor; an agent must have
        // a corresponding person object.
        public Agent(Person aPerson) {
            // implicit call to superclass constructor super();
            this.person = aPerson; }
✂
}
```

Code notes: Each passenger object and agent object requires a corresponding person object. Therefore, for Passenger and Agent, this code creates a constructor that requires a person object, but it purposely does not provide a default constructor.

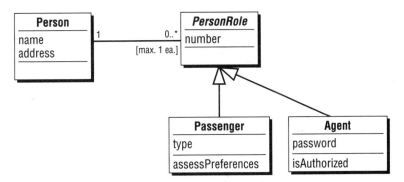

Figure 2-11. A person and its roles (composition); roles and special kinds of roles (inheritance).

2.4 Example: Both Composition and Inheritance

Yes, passenger and agent are special kinds of person roles.

So, you can apply composition (person and its roles) in tandem with inheritance (person roles and special kinds of person roles), as shown in Figure 2-11.

When you check the inheritance usage criteria this time, you find:

1. "Is a special kind of," not "is a role played by a"

    Pass. Passenger and agent are special kinds of person roles (not roles that a "person role" plays).

2. Never needs to transmute to be an object in some other class

    Pass. A passenger object forever stays a passenger object; there is no need to transmute it to an object in some other class; the same is true for agent.

3. Extends rather than overrides or nullifies

    Pass. Both subclasses extend the responsibilities defined in the superclass.

4. Does not subclass what is merely a utility class

    Pass. Okay here.

5. Within PD: Expresses special kinds of roles, transactions, or things.

    Pass. Now we have special kinds of roles. All is well.

A nice combination! Cool.

In Java, it looks like this:

```
public class Person {

    // attributes / private / associations
    private Vector roles = new Vector();
    // methods / public / accessors for association values
    public void addRole(PersonRole aRole) {
        this.roles.addElement( aRole); }
    public void removeRole(PersonRole aRole) {
        this.roles.removeElement(aRole); }
    public Enumeration getRoles() {
        return this.roles.elements(); }

}
```

Code notes: The above code does not check for an existing role when a role is added. That is, a person can add many agent roles to its list of roles.

```
public abstract class PersonRole {

    // attributes / private / associations
    protected Person person;

    // methods / public / accessors for association values
    public Person getPerson() { return this.person; }

    // constructors
    // note that there is no *default* constructor; a person role must have
    // a corresponding person object.
    public PersonRole(Person aPerson) {
        // implicit call to superclass constructor super();
        this.person = aPerson; }
```

```
✂
}

public class Passenger extends PersonRole {
✂
    // constructors
    // notice that there is no *default* superclass constructor;
    // an explicit call to the superclass constructor is required.
    public Passenger(Person aPerson) { super( aPerson); }
✂
}
public class Agent extends PersonRole {
✂
    // constructors
    // notice that there is no *default* superclass constructor;
    // an explicit call to the superclass constructor is required.
    public Agent(Person aPerson) { super( aPerson); }
✂
}
```

Code notes: Since Java implicitly creates a default constructor for a class with-out a constructor, and since the default constructor includes an implicit call to the superclass' default constructor, both Passenger and Agent require a con-structor that calls PersonRole's nondefault constructor.

2.5 Example: Inheritance (the Exception)

Consider an example for Charlie's Charters. Suppose that you ex-pand the context for the moment to include both reservations and purchases.

Extend the responsibilities expressed by the model to include pur-chases. You have two special kinds of transactions to deal with: reservation and purchase. Add a generalization class, called "trans-action." Then extend it with two specialization classes, reservation and purchase.

Now you have two special kinds of transactions (moments or inter-vals of time): reservation and purchase. Some reservation objects will have a corresponding purchase object.

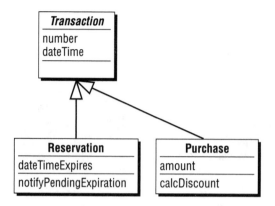

Figure 2-12.   Special kinds of transactions.

Figure 2-12 illustrates this concept.

But is this a good use of inheritance? After all, we could use composition (see Figure 2-13).

However, we'd like to get the benefit of inheritance in those special cases where it is applicable. After all, explicitly capturing commonality in a class diagram and in source code is a very attractive thing.

So check out this use of inheritance, using the five-part checklist:

1. "Is a special kind of," not "is a role played by a"

    Pass. Reservation is a special kind of Transaction (not a role that a transaction plays); Purchase is a special kind of Transaction (not a role that a transaction plays).

2. Never needs to transmute to be an object in some other class

    Pass. A reservation object stays a reservation object, even if we create a corresponding purchase object at some point along the way. In fact, a reservation object might need to know its corresponding purchase object. (Egad! That means composition between objects in the subclasses. Composition is indeed the norm; it is nearly everywhere.)

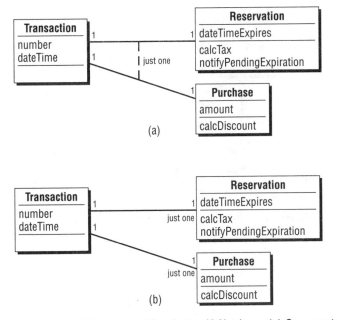

Figure 2-13. Use composition instead? Not here. (a) One way to show "just one." (b) Another way to show "just one."

3. Extends rather than overrides or nullifies

   Pass. Reservation extends the definition of Transaction (adding the dateTimeExpires attribute and the notifyPendingExpiration method); Purchase extends the definition of Transaction (adding the amount attribute and the calcDiscount method).

4. Does not subclass what is merely a utility class

   Pass. Okay here.

5. Within PD: Expresses special kinds of roles, transactions, or things.

   Pass. Here, it's special kinds of transactions.

We could use both inheritance and composition here:

- inheritance—for special kinds of transactions

- composition—a reservation object is composed of a corresponding purchase object.

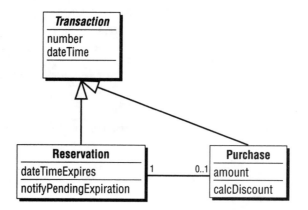

Figure 2-14.   Inheritance with a little composition too.

See Figure 2-14 for the result.

Here's how it looks in Java:

```java
public class Transaction {
✂
    // attributes / private
    protected int number;
    protected Date dateTime;

    // methods / public / accessors for attribute values
    public int getNumber() { return this.number; }
    public void setNumber(int aNumber) { this.number = aNumber; }
    public Date getDate() { return this.dateTime; }
    public void setDate(Date aDateTime) { this.dateTime = aDateTime; }
✂
}

public class Reservation extends Transaction {
✂
    // attributes / private
    private Date dateTimeExpires;

    // attributes / private / associations
    private Purchase purchase;
```

```
            // methods / public / accessors for attribute values
            public Date getDateTimeExpires() { return this.dateTimeExpires; }
            public void setDateTimeExpires(Date aDateTime) {
                this.dateTimeExpires = aDateTime; }

            // methods / public / accessors for association values
            public void addPurchase(Purchase aPurchase) {
                this.purchase = aPurchase; }
            public void removePurchase() { this.purchase = null; }
            public Purchase getPurchase() { return this.purchase; }
        ✂
        }


public class Purchase extends Transaction {
✂
            // attributes / private
            private float amount;
            // attributes / private / associations
            private Reservation reservation;

            // methods / public / accessors for attribute values
            public float getAmount() { return this.amount; }
            public void setAmount(float anAmount) { this.amount = anAmount; }

            // methods / public / accessors for association values
            public Reservation getReservation() { return this.reservation; }

            // constructors
            // note that there is no *default* constructor; a purchase must have
            // a corresponding reservation.
            public Purchase(Reservation aReservation) {
                // implicit call to superclass constructor super();
                this.reservation = aReservation; }
        ✂
        }
```

2.6   Example: Inheritance in Need of Adjustment

Consider another possibility. Switch over to Zoe's Zones for this one.

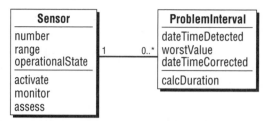

Figure 2-15. A sensor and its problem intervals.

Remember the sensor class? Figure 2-15 illustrates this as well as the association to some number of problem intervals, to round out this example.

Now we find out that we will be working with remote sensors too. Instead of activating and monitoring a remote sensor, all we can do is request a reading from it (getting back a value and its operational state).

Extend the responsibilities expressed by the model to include a new kind of sensor. Extend the Sensor class with one specialization class, RemoteSensor.

You could add a subclass (Figure 2-16).

But for a remote sensor object you don't need an association to a problem interval. Nor do we need activate, monitor, or assess for interacting with a remote sensor. The X's in the figure mark the things a remote sensor nullifies; they're not needed, and are never used.

Maybe we were a bit hasty in subclassing. Was this a good use of inheritance? Pull out the checklist one more time:

1. "Is a special kind of," not "is a role played by a"

   Pass. Remote Sensor is a special kind of Sensor (not a role that a sensor plays)

2. Never needs to transmute to be an object in some other class

   Pass. A remote sensor remains a remote sensor that is not under our direct control.

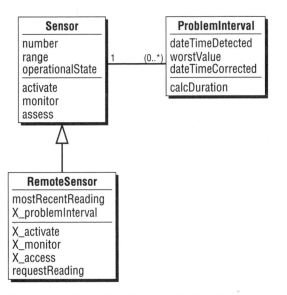

Figure 2-16. Extending Sensor with RemoteSensor.

3. Extends, rather than overrides or nullifies

Fail. Ahhh, here's the catch. The remote sensor class nullifies, has no use for an association to problem interval or the method trio (activate, monitor, assess).

4. Does not subclass what is merely a utility class

Pass. Okay here.

5. Within PD: Expresses special kinds of roles, transactions, or things.

Pass. Here, it's a special kind of thing (a device).

You're close. Inheritance does apply, you just need to rearrange the hierarchy a bit.

Try this: Extend the responsibilities expressed by the model to include activatable sensors and remote sensors. You have two special kinds of sensors to deal with: activatable sensors and remote sensors. You can keep a generalization class, called "sensor." Then you can extend it with two specialization classes, activatable sensor and remote sensor (Figure 2-17). The ProblemInterval remains associated only at the ActivatableSensor level.

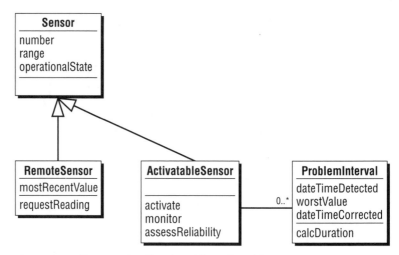

Figure 2-17.   Rearranging the class hierarchy a bit.

Now checklist criterion number 3 is satisfied (extends, rather than nullifies) along with the others. You've made it—good inheritance!

2.7   Example: Thread

Suppose you want to add a thread (a copy of a program, running with the same data as other copies of that program) to an object model.

Is it time for composition, or inheritance? (See Figure 2-18.)

In Java, it looks like this:

```
public class Sensor extends Thread {

    // attributes / private
    private int number;
    private int range;
    // methods / public / override
    public void run () { /* code goes here */ }

}
```

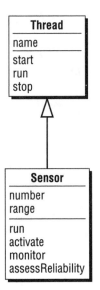

Figure 2-18.   A kind of thread?

Again, consider the exception: inheritance. Is a sensor a kind of thread? Does specialization apply here?

1. "Is a special kind of," not "is a role played by a"

   Fail. A sensor is not a kind of thread.

2. Never needs to transmute to be an object in some other class

   Pass. Okay here.

3. Extends, rather than overrides or nullifies

   Pass. Okay here.

4. Does not subclass what is merely a utility class

   Pass. Okay here.

5. Within PD: Expresses special kinds of roles, transactions, or things.

   Not applicable (Thread is an infrastructure class, not a PD class)

Composition to the rescue. Here's how it works. The Java runtime system manages threads. Define a sensor class with a "run" method. Create a sensor object. Create a thread object. Finally, send the sensor object to the thread object, asking it to run what you pass to it.

Extend the responsibilities of a sensor object with a thread object (see Figure 2-19).

The Thread class comes with Java. Here's what the Sensor class looks like in Java:

```
public class Sensor implements Runnable {
✂
    // attributes / private
    private int number;
    private int range;

    // attributes / private / associations
    private Thread monitorThread;
    private Thread assessThread;

    // methods / public / Runnable implementation
    public void run() { /* code goes here */ }
✂
}
```

We'll spend more time on threads in Chapter 4.

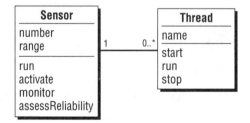

Figure 2-19. A sensor and its threads.

2.8   Example: Applet

Now take a look at the Applet class in Java.

Inheritance chain: Applet is a special kind of Panel is a special kind of Container is a special kind of Component is a special kind of Object (Figure 2-20).

Is this a good use of inheritance? Check it out:

1.   "Is a special kind of," not "is a role played by a"

Pass. Applet is a special kind of Panel, is a special kind of Container, is a special kind of Component, is a special kind of Object—not a role played.

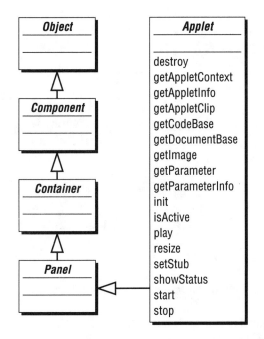

Figure 2-20.   Applet and its superclasses.

2. Never needs to transmute to be an object in some other class

    Pass. An applet remains an applet.

3. Extends, rather than overrides or nullifies

    Pass. An applet extends what a panel is all about.

4. Does not subclass what is merely a utility class

    Pass. Okay here.

5. Within PD: Expresses special kinds of roles, transactions, or things.

    Not applicable (applet is an infrastructure class, not a PD class)

So, yes, this is a good use of inheritance.

When we extend (inherit from) Applet, we get all the goodies for gluing together what we need in an applet. Typically,

- we use some methods as they are (for example: getAudioClip, getImage, play)
- other methods are specific to our applet (for example: init, start, resize, stop, destroy).

What happens when you want to add your own special kind of applet? Whoops! By now, the wording of that question should tip you off—"a special kind of."

Add specializations that are indeed special kinds of applets, for example, a "ReservationUI" applet. Extend the responsibilities of the applet class with inheritance (see Figure 2-21).

Here's what it looks like in Java:

```
public class ReservationUI_Applet extends Applet {
✂

    // methods / public / Applet override
    public void init() {
        /* initialization code goes here */ }
✂

}
```

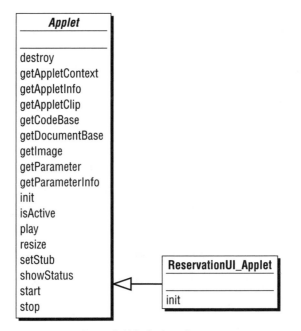

Figure 2-21. A special kind of applet.

2.9 Example: Observable

Now consider the Observable class in Java (see Figure 2-22).

Observable is a class that is used in notification. Or at least, it is supposed to be used that way.

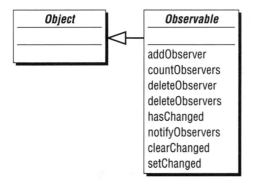

Figure 2-22. Observable and its superclass.

Observable consists of a number of methods that make it easier for an observable object to notify other objects about a state change.

Suppose that you make Reservation a subclass of Observable, so it acts as an observable (see Figure 2-23). That way, a reservation object can notify other objects (notably UI objects) whenever it changes.

Is this a good use of inheritance? Check it out:

1. "Is a special kind of," not "is a role played by a"

   Fail. A reservation is not a special kind of observable. (Well, maybe, in a real abstract sense. Somehow it doesn't feel right. Let's check the other criteria.)

2. Never needs to transmute to be an object in some other class

   Pass. A reservation object remains a reservation object.

3. Extends, rather than overrides or nullifies

   Pass. Reservation extends what Observable is all about.

4. Does not subclass what is merely a utility class

   Fail. Observable is a utility class, a collection of useful methods—nothing more.

5. Within PD: Expresses special kinds of roles, transactions, or things.

   Not applicable (Observable is a utility class, not a PD class).

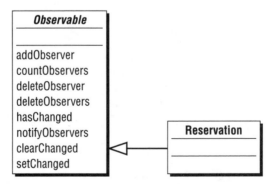

Figure 2-23.   A special kind of observable.

So inheritance does *not* apply here, even though it's set up that way in Java.

Don't worry, though. A subsequent chapter presents several very useful alternatives.

2.10 Summary

You've explored two mechanisms for extending a design: composition and inheritance.

Inheritance is useful in limited contexts. Composition is useful in nearly every context (see Figure 2-24).

Inheritance was all the rage in the early days of object-oriented development. But over time, designers have discovered that inheritance is effective only within certain contexts.

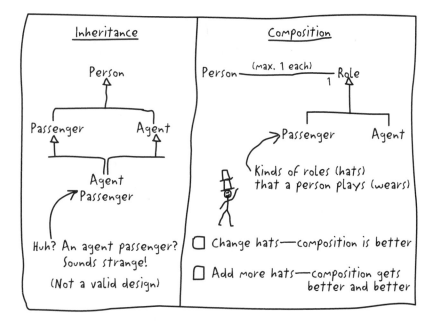

Figure 2-24.   Summary: inheritance vs. composition.

Composition, in tandem with interfaces (Chapter 3), is far more common, far more generally useful, and much closer to the heart of good object-oriented design.

Here are the strategies that you've learned and applied in this chapter:

Composition Strategy: *Use Composition to extend responsibilities by delegating work to other objects.*

When to Inherit Strategy: *Inheritance is used to extend attributes and methods; but encapsulation is weak within a class hierarchy, so use of this mechanism is limited. Use it when you can satisfy the following criteria:*

1. *"Is a special kind of," not "is a role played by a"*

2. *Never needs to transmute to be an object in some other class*

3. *Extends rather than overrides or nullifies superclass*

4. *Does not subclass what is merely a utility class (useful functionality you'd like to reuse)*

5. *Within PD: expresses special kinds of roles, transactions, or things*

Chapter 3

Design with Interfaces

This chapter explores Java-style interfaces: what they are, why they are important, and how and when to use them.

3.1   What Are Interfaces?

Interfaces are the key to pluggability, the ability to remove one component and replace it with another. Consider the electrical outlets in your home: The interface is well-defined (plug shape, receptacle shape, voltage level, polarity for each prong); you can readily unplug a toaster and plug in a java-maker, and continue on your merry way.

Design with interfaces? Yes!

An *interface* is a collection of method signatures that you define for use again and again in your application. It's a listing of method signatures alone. There is neither a common description, nor any source code behind these method signatures.*

An interface describes a standard protocol, a standard way of interacting with objects in classes that implement the interface.

Working with interfaces requires that you (1) specify the interface and (2) specify which classes implement that interface.

Begin with a simple interface, called IName (Figure 3-1). IName consists of two method signatures, the accessors getName and setName.

---

*Java expresses inheritance and polymorphism distinctly with different syntax. C++ expresses both concepts with a single syntax; it blurs the distinction between these very different mechanisms, resulting in overly complex, overly deep class hierarchies. (We design with interfaces regardless of language; Java makes it easier for us to express that design in source code.)

In Smalltalk, interfaces (called protocols) are agreed upon by convention and learned by reading source code. In C++, interfaces are implemented as classes with no default implementation (everything inside is declared as being "pure virtual").

Java interfaces can also include constants. This provides a convenient way to package useful constants when programming, but it has no impact on effective design.

Within the Java Language Specification, a signature is defined in a narrower way, describing what a Java compiler must pay attention to when resolving overloaded methods. In that document, an interface consists of a method name and the number and types of parameters—not the return type, not the name of the parameters, and not any thrown exceptions. For overridden methods (in an extending/ implementing class, using the same method name and the same number and types of parameters), a Java compiler checks to make sure that the return type is the same and the thrown exceptions are the same.

UML offers a definition with the same basic meaning as the one we use in this book: "An interface is a declaration of a collection of operations that may be used for defining a service offered by an instance."

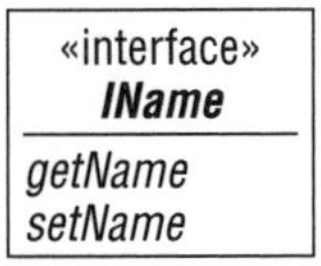

```
«interface»
  IName
getName
setName
```

Figure 3-1. An interface.

By convention, interface names are capitalized: the IName interface. References to an object of a class that implements an interface are not capitalized: a name object, meaning, an object in a class that implements IName.

By one convention, interface names end with the suffix "-able," "-ible," or (occasionally) "-er."*

By another convention, interface names begin with the prefix "I."

By convention in this book, interface names begin with the prefix "I" and are followed by

- a noun, if it's an accessor interface

- a verb, if it's a calculation interface, or

- a noun or a verb, if it's a combination of interfaces.**

In Figure 3-1 the interface name is "I" + a noun.

---

*Requiring interface names to end in -able or -ible is a bit too complicated a convention. However, if you'd like to adopt this convention, take note of the following English-language spelling rules:

1. Drop a silent "e" before adding "-able."

2. Check a dictionary. If the spelling is not listed, look at other forms of the word to see which letter might make sense. (Again, this is a bit too complicated for day-to-day use.)

**Choose whatever prefix convention you prefer: I, I_, Int_; whatever. We prefer "I" (as long as it does not conflict with other prefix conventions of the project).

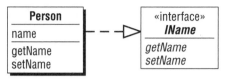

Figure 3-2.   A class that promises to implement the IName interface.

In Java, an IName interface might look something like this:

```
public interface IName {
    String getName();
    voidsetName(String aName); }
```

A class that implements the IName interface promises to implement the "get name" and "set name" methods in a way that is appropriate for that class. The "get name" method returns the name of an object. The "set name" method establishes a new name for an object (Figure 3-2). A dashed arrow indicates that a class (at the tail of the arrow) implements the interface (at the head of the arrow).

The IName interface describes a standard way to interact with an object in any class that implements that interface.

This means that as an object in any class, you could hold an IName object (that is, objects within any number of classes that implement the IName interface). And you could ask an IName object for its name without knowing or caring about what class that object happens to be in.

3.2   Why Use Interfaces?

3.2.1   The Problem

Over the years, you may have encountered the classic barrier to:

- flexibility (graciously accommodating changes in direction)
- extensibility (graciously accommodating add-ons), and
- pluggability (graciously accommodating pulling out one class of objects and inserting another with the same method signatures).

Yes, this is a barrier within object-oriented design.

All objects interact with other objects to get something done. An object can answer a question or calculate a result all by itself, but even then some other object does the asking. In short, objects interact with other objects. That's why scenario views are so significant, because they model time-ordered sequences of interactions between objects.

The problem with most class diagrams and scenarios is that an object must be within a specified class.

Yet what is the element of reuse? It's not just a class. After all, objects in a class are interconnected with objects in other classes. The element of reuse is some number of classes, the number of classes in a scenario, or even more, the total number of classes contained in overlapping scenarios.

What's the impact, in terms of pluggability? If you want to add another class of objects, one that can be plugged in as a substitute for an object in another class already in a scenario, you are in trouble. There is no pluggability here. Instead, you must add associations, build another scenario, and implement source code behind it all.*

The problem is that each association and each message-send is hardwired to objects in a specific class (or class hierarchy), impeding pluggability, as well as extensibility and flexibility.

Traditionally, objects in a scenario are hardwired to each other. But if the "who I know" (associations) and "who I interact with" (messages) are hardwired to just one class of objects, then pluggability is nonexistent; adding a new class means adding the class itself, associations, and scenarios, in addition to making changes to other classes in the design and in source code.

---

*In C++, developers often implement monolithic class hierarchies with a base class that does nothing more than allow the ease of "pluggability" via base class pointers. This is a bulky and limited workaround compared to the elegance of Java interfaces.

3.2.2   A Partial Solution

We'd like a more flexible, extensible, and pluggable approach, one that would let us add in new classes of objects with no change in associations or message-sends.

There is a partial solution.

If you want to add a new class that is a subclass of one of the classes of objects participating in a scenario, you can do so without any problems. Show the generalization class in your scenario, add a note indicating that any object in a specialization class will do, and you are ready to go.

However, if inheritance does not apply, or if you have already used inheritance in some other way (keeping in mind that Java is a single inheritance language), then this partial solution is no solution at all.

3.2.3   Flexibility, Extensibility, and Pluggability—That's Why

Interfaces enhance, facilitate, and even make possible the flexibility, extensibility, and pluggability that we so desire.

Interfaces shift one's thinking about an object and its associations and interactions with other objects.

Challenge Each Association Strategy: Is this association hardwired only to objects in that class (simpler), or is this an association to any object that implements a certain interface (more flexible, extensible, pluggable)?

For an object and its associations to other objects ask, "Is this association hardwired only to objects in that class, or is this an association to any object that implements a certain interface?" If it's the latter, you are in effect saying, "I don't care what kind of object I am associated with, just as long as that object implements the interface that I need."

Interfaces also shift one's thinking about an object and the kinds of objects that it interacts with during a scenario.

Challenge Each Message-Send Strategy: *Is this message-send hardwired only to objects in that class (simpler), or is this a message-send to any object that implements a certain interface (more flexible, extensible, pluggable)?*

For each message-send to another object ask, "Is this message-send hardwired only to objects in that class, or is this a message-send to any object that implements a certain interface? If it's the latter, you are in effect saying, "I don't care what kind of object I am sending messages to, just as long as that object implements the interface that I need."

So, when you need flexibility, specify associations (in class diagrams) and message-sends (in scenarios) to objects in *any* class that implements the interface that is needed, rather than to objects in a *single* class (or its subclasses).

Interfaces loosen up coupling, make parts of a design more interchangeable, and increase the likelihood of reuse—all for a modest increase in design complexity.

Interfaces express "is a kind of" in a very limited way, "is a kind that supports this interface." This gives you the categorization benefits of inheritance; at the same time, it obviates the major weakness of inheritance: weak encapsulation within a class hierarchy.

Interfaces give composition a much broader sphere of influence. With interfaces, composition is flexible, extensible, and pluggable (composed of objects that implement an interface), rather than hardwired to just one kind of object (composed of objects in just one class).

Interfaces reduce the otherwise compelling need to jam many, many classes into a class hierarchy with lots of multiple inheritance. In effect, using interfaces streamlines how one uses inheritance: use interfaces to express generalization-specialization of method signatures (behavior); use inheritance to express general-ization-specialization of interfaces implemented—along with addi-tional attributes and methods.

Interfaces give you a way to separate method signatures from method implementations. So you can use them to separate UI method signatures from operating-system dependent method im-plementations; that's exactly what Java's Abstract Windowing Toolkit (AWT) and Swing do. You can do the same for data manage-ment, separating method signatures from vendor-dependent method implementations. You can also do the same for problem-domain objects, as you'll see later in this chapter.

Sound-bite summary: Why use interfaces? Interfaces give us a way to establish associations and message-sends to objects in any class that implements a needed interface, without hardwiring associations or hardwiring message-sends to a specific class of objects.

The larger the system and the longer the potential life span of a sys-tem, the more significant interfaces become.

3.3 Factor-out Interfaces

Factoring out every method signature into a separate interface would be overkill—you'd make your object models more complex and your scenarios way too abstract.

In what contexts should you apply interfaces?

You can factor out method signatures into interfaces in a variety of contexts, but the following are the four contexts in which inter-faces really help:

> Factor out repeaters.
>
> Factor out to a proxy.

Factor out for analogous apps.

Factor out for future expansion.

3.3.1   Factor Out Repeaters

Begin with the simplest use of interfaces: to factor out common method signatures to bring a higher level of abstraction (and an overall visual simplification) to a class diagram. This is a modest yet important use of interfaces.

Factor Out Repeaters Strategy: Factor out method signatures that repeat within your class diagram. Resolve synonyms into a single signature. Generalize overly specific names into a single signature. Reasons for use: to explicitly capture the common, reusable behavior and to bring a higher level of abstraction into the model.

Look for repeating method signatures and factor them out.

Example: calcTotal in one class, calcTotal in another class.

Factor out that method signature into an ITotal interface.

Mark each class as one that implements the ITotal interface.

Now look for method signatures that are synonyms. Pick a common method signature and factor it out.

Example: calcTotal in one class, determineTotalAmount in another class. Same behavior.

Pick a synonym: calcTotal.

Factor out that method signature into an ITotal interface.

Mark each class as one that implements the ITotal interface.

Next take each method signature and generalize it. (But be careful not to generalize to the point of obscurity; a method name like "process it" or "calculate it" would not be very helpful, would it?)

Then look for method signatures that are synonyms; finally, pick a common method signature and factor it out.

> Example: calcSubtotal in one class, calcTotal in another class, calcGrandTotal in another class.
>
> Pick a synonym: calcTotal.
>
> Factor out that method signature into an ITotal interface.
>
> Mark each class as one that implements the ITotal interface.

When factoring out interfaces, you also need to consider the return types and the parameter types; they must match up, too. In fact in a class diagram, you could include a complete method signature:

> return type + method name + parameter types + exceptions

However, including all of that information in a class diagram takes up far too much screen real estate. It is far better to have an effective class diagram of the design plus source code with fine-grained details, side by side.

3.3.1.1 Example: The Lunch Counter at Charlie's Charters

Okay then, apply the "Factor Our Repeaters" strategy. Consider a point-of-sale application for the lunch counter at Charlie's Charters.

Build an initial class diagram (Figure 3-3).

In Java, it looks like this:

```
public class Customer {
✂

    // methods / public / conducting business
    public BigDecimal howMuch() { /* code goes here */ }
✂

}
```

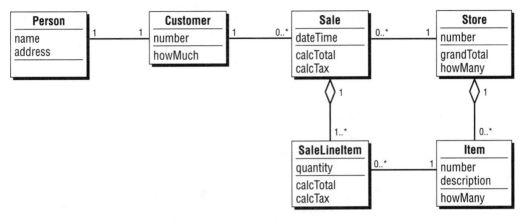

Figure 3-3. Repeating method signatures.

```
public class Sale {

    // methods / public / conducting business
    public BigDecimal calcTotal() { /* code goes here */ }
    public BigDecimal calcTax() { /* code goes here */ }

}
public class SaleLineItem {

    // methods / public / conducting business
    public BigDecimal calcTotal() { /* code goes here */ }
    public BigDecimal calcTax() { /* code goes here */ }

}
public class Store {

    // methods / public / conducting business
    public BigDecimal grandTotal() { /* code goes here */ }
    public int howMany() { /* code goes here */ }

}
public class Item {

    // methods / public / conducting business
```

```
    public int howMany() { /* code goes here */ }
✂
}
```

Applying the "factor out repeaters" strategy:

You can factor out calcTotal without any problem.

Now look for synonyms.

The methods calcTotal and howMany could be synonyms, but they have distinct meanings here (adding monetary units versus tallying some items, respectively).

Moreover, the return types don't match. This is a problem. We could check the return types to see if they too are synonyms; or we could try generalizing each return type to see if that helps. In this case, however, calcTotal returns a BigDecimal number; howMany returns an integer. You cannot combine different method signatures into a single interface method signature.

Keep looking. The calcTotal and howMuch methods are synonyms, and the return types match (both return a BigDecimal value). One or the other will do just fine; choose calcTotal and factor it out.

Looking further, grandTotal is a specialized name for calcTotal. Use calcTotal for both.

What are the common method signatures? Let's see:

- howMany—occurs twice
- calcTax—occurs twice
- calcTotal, how much (synonyms here)—occurs four times.

You can factor out those common method signatures, using these interfaces:

- ICount—how many
- ITax—calcTax
- ITotal—calcTotal.

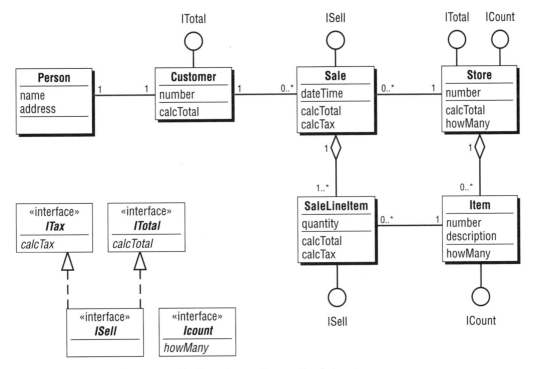

Figure 3-4. Factor out repeating method signatures.

You can go a step further. What common interface combinations are we using?

- ITotal, ITax—occur together, twice.

So you can combine those two interfaces, with this result:

- ISell—ITotal, ITax.

The result? See Figure 3-4. The "lollipops" indicate interface implementers. Another way to indicate interface implementers is with implement links, dashed arrows from implementers to interfaces. Convention: use interface links until they overpower your class diagram, then switch over to lollipops to avoid link overload.

In Java, it looks like this:

```
public interface ICount {
     int howMany(); }

public interface ITotal {
     BigDecimal calcTotal(); }

public interface ITax {
     BigDecimal calcTax(); }

public interface ISell extends ITotal, ITax {}
public class Customer implements ITotal {
✂
     // methods / public / ITotal implementation
     public BigDecimal calcTotal() { /* code goes here */ }
✂
}
public class Sale implements ISell {
✂
     // methods / public / ISell implementation
     public BigDecimal calcTotal() { /* code goes here */ }
     public BigDecimal calcTax() { /* code goes here */ }
✂
}
public class SaleLineItem implements ISell {
✂
     // methods / public / ISell implementation
     public BigDecimal calcTotal() { /* code goes here */ }
     public BigDecimal calcTax() { /* code goes here */ }
✂
}
public class Store implements ITotal, ICount {
✂
     // methods / public / ITotal implementation
     public BigDecimal calcTotal() { /* code goes here */ }
     // methods / public / ICount implementation
     public int howMany() { /* code goes here */ }
✂
}
```

```
public class Item implements ICount {

    // methods / public / ICount implementation
    public int howMany() { /* code goes here */ }

}
```

Especially note this:

```
public interface ISell extends ITotal, ITax {}
```

Here, an interface extends two other interfaces. Is this Multiple inheritance?

Well, yes and no.

Yes, the new interface is a combination of the other two interfaces. Yes, ISell is a special kind of ITotal and a special kind of ITax.

No, it's not inheritance; only method signatures are involved. There is absolutely no implementation behind these method signatures.

We really don't think of it as inheritance, either.

We think of interfaces as useful method-signature descriptions, ones that we can conveniently mix and match with the "extends" keyword to provide pluggability.

One way to visualize it is to picture a stack of index cards; each card has an interface name and its method signatures on it; grab whatever combination is useful to you (ITotal, ITax); name that useful combination (ISell)—especially if it is reusable.

3.3.1.2 Example: Simplify and Identify Object-Model Patterns

Together with David North, we have cataloged 31 object-model patterns: templates of objects with stereotypical responsibilities and interactions. Those patterns are documented at www.oi.com/handbook and (more thoroughly) in the book, *Object Models: Strategies, Patterns, and Applications*.

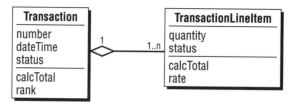

Figure 3-5. The transaction-transaction line item object-model pattern.

One of the more puzzling matters has been how to show these patterns within source code. Some have proposed adding extra classes of objects to manage each pattern, but that seemed like overkill somehow.

Interfaces offer an interesting twist. And the simplest use of interfaces, factoring out common method signatures, takes on some added significance.

Consider the transaction pattern called "transaction–transaction line item" (Figure 3-5).

Other patterns use attributes and methods with exactly the same names. So everything can be factored out into interfaces.

For full impact, first add in attribute accessors (Figure 3-6).

In Java, it looks like this:

```
public class Transaction {

    // attributes / private
    private int number;
    private Date dateTime;
    private String status;

    // attributes / private / associations
    private Vector transactionLineItems = new Vector();

    // methods / public / conducting business
    public float calcTotal() { /* code goes here */ }
```

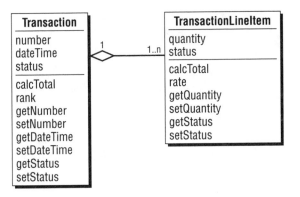

Figure 3-6. An object-model pattern with attribute accessors.

```
public Enumeration rank() {
    /* return an enumeration with ranked transaction line items */
    /* code goes here */ }

// methods / public / accessors for attribute values
public int getNumber() { return this.number; }
public void setNumber(int aNumber) { this.number = aNumber; }
public Date getDateTime() { return this.dateTime; }
public void setDateTime(Date aDateTime)
    { this.dateTime = aDateTime; }
public String getStatus() { return this.status; }
public void setStatus(String aStatus) { this.status = aStatus; }
```
✂
```
}


public class TransactionLineItem {
```
✂
```
    // attributes / private
    private int quantity;
    private String status;

    // attributes / private / associations
    private Transaction transaction;

    // methods / public / conducting business
    public float calcTotal() { /* code goes here */ }
    public int rate() { /* code goes here */ }
```

```
// methods / public / accessors for attribute values
public int getQuantity() { return this.quantity; }
public void setQuantity(int aQuantity) { this.quantity = aQuantity; }
public String getStatus() { return this.status; }
public void setStatus(String aStatus) { this.status = aStatus; }
✂
}
```

Second, apply the "factor out repeaters" strategy (Figure 3-7).

In Java, it looks like this:

```
public interface IRank {
    Enumeration rank(); }
```

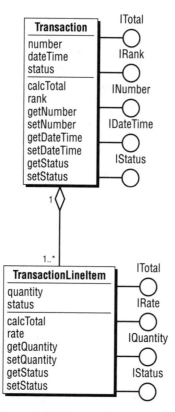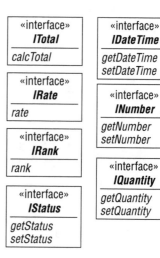

Figure 3-7. Factor out repeaters.

```
public interface IRate {
    int rate(); }

public interface ITotal {
    float calcTotal() ; }

public interface INumber {
    int getNumber();
    void setNumber(int aNumber); }

public interface IDateTime {
    Date getDateTime();
    void setDateTime(Date aDate); }

public interface IQuantity {
    int getQuantity();
    void setQuantity(int aQuantity); }

public interface IStatus {
    String getStatus();
    void setStatus(String aStatus); }

public class Transaction
    implements IRank, ITotal, INumber, IDateTime, IStatus {

        // class definition here

}

public class TransactionLineItem
    implements IRate, ITotal, IQuantity, IStatus {

        // class definition here

}
```

Now, go for the gold: factor out the interfaces within each "pattern player," making pattern players explicit in the design (and ultimately, in source code). See Figure 3-8.

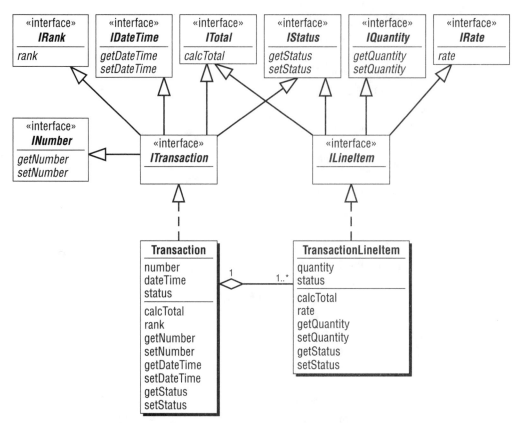

Figure 3-8. Factor out completely, so you can mark out pattern players.

In Java, it looks like this:

```
public interface ITransaction
        extends ITotal, IRank, INumber, IDateTime, IStatus {}

public interface ILineItem
        extends ITotal, IRate, IQuantity, IStatus {}

public class Transaction implements ITransaction {
```

```
✂
        // class definition here
✂
}

public class TransactionLineItem implements ILineItem {
✂
        // class definition here
✂
}
```

3.3.2   Factor Out to a Proxy

Factor Out to a Proxy Strategy: *Factor out method signatures into a proxy, an object with a solo association to some other object. Reason for use: to simplify the proxy within a class diagram and its scenarios (Figure 3-9).*

3.3.2.1 Recognizing a Proxy

Another way to bring interfaces into your design is to factor out method signatures into a proxy. A proxy is one who acts as a substitute on behalf of another. Consider person and passenger in Charlie's Charters' reservation system, this time with get and set accessors included (Figure 3-9).

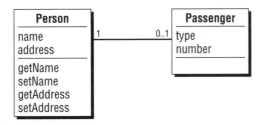

Figure 3-9.   Person with accessors.

In Java, it looks like this:

```java
public class Person {

    // attributes / private
    private String name;
    private String address;

    // attributes / private / associations
    private Passenger passenger;

    // methods / public / accessors for attribute values
    public String getName() { return this.name; }
    public void setName(String aName) { this.name = aName; }
    public String getAddress() { return this.address; }
    public void setAddress(String anAddress)
        { this.address = anAddress; }

    // methods / public / accessors for association values
    public void addPassenger(Passenger aPassenger) {
        this.passenger = aPassenger; }
    public void removePassenger() { this.passenger = null; }
    public Passenger getPassenger() { return this.passenger; }

}

public class Passenger {

    // attributes / private
    private int number;
    private String type;

    // attributes / private / associations
    private Person person;

    // methods / public / accessors for attribute values
    public String getNumber() { return this.number; }
    public void setNumber(int aNumber) { this.number = aNumber; }
    public String getType() { return this.type; }
    public void setType(String aType)
        { this.type = aType; }
```

```
// methods / public / accessors for association values
public Person getPerson() { return this.person; }

// constructors
// notice that there is no *default* constructor; a passenger must have
// a corresponding person object.
public Passenger(Person aPerson) {
    // implicit call to superclass constructor super();
    this.person = aPerson; }
✂
}
```

Passenger has a "one and only one" association with a person ob-ject. Whenever an object (Passenger) has a "one and only one" asso-ciation with another object (Person), then that object (Passenger) can act as a proxy for the other (Person).

3.3.2.2 Life without a Proxy

Proxy? Why bother? Well, consider this "before" picture, where you don't have one object acting as a proxy for another. Suppose that you've identified a passenger object, and would like to know its name and address. What does the scenario look like? Ask a pas-senger, delegate to a person—explicitly. Again and again. There must be a better way to deal with this (Figure 3-10.)

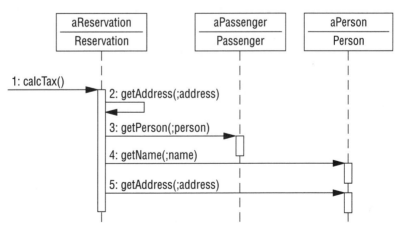

Figure 3-10. Asking a passenger for its person object, then asking a person ob-ject for its name and address.

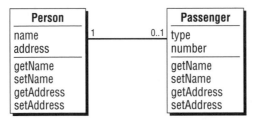

Figure 3-11.   Person and Passenger, both with accessors.

3.3.2.3 Life with a Proxy

A proxy answers questions on behalf of another, and it provides a convenient interface. See Figure 3-11.

A proxy-based scenario is shown in Figure 3-12.

In Java, it looks like this:

```
public class Passenger {
✂
    // methods / public / accessors for Person's attribute values
    public String getName() { return this.person.getName(); }
    public void setName(String aName) { this.person.setName(aName); }
    public String getAddress() { return this.person.getAddress(); }
```

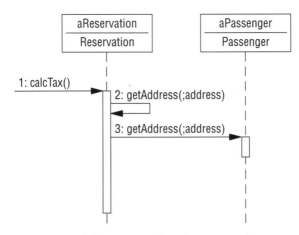

Figure 3-12.   Asking a proxy for what you need.

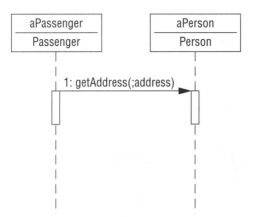

Figure 3-13. Behind the scene: a proxy interacting with the one it represents (boring).

```
public void setAddress(String anAddress)
    { this.person.setAddress(anAddress); }

}
```

Now you can ask a passenger for its name and address rather than asking a passenger for its person object and then interacting with that person object.

Yes, a passenger object still privately interacts with its person object. We could show that interaction, as illustrated in a separate scenario view (Figure 3-13).

But that really is rather boring and not something we would normally sketch out.

Hence, with a proxy, scenarios become simpler; the details about whomever is being represented by the proxy are shielded from view, letting the important stand out, improving effective communication—a good thing.

3.3.2.4 Introducing a Proxy Interface

Now let's bring interfaces into the picture. Factoring out commonality yields Figure 3-14.

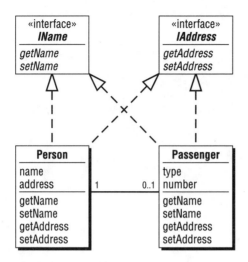

Figure 3-14.   Person and Passenger, with common interfaces.

In Java, it looks like this:

```
public interface IName {
      String getName();
      void setName(String aName);
}

public interface IAddress {
      String getAddress();
      void setAddress(String anAddress);
}

public class Person implements IName, IAddress {
✀
      // class definition here
✀
}

public class Passenger implements IName, IAddress {
✀
      // class definition here
✀
}
```

You can combine these two interfaces as shown in Figure 3-15.

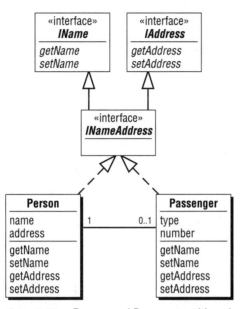

Figure 3-15.   Person and Passenger with a single, combined interface.

In Java, it looks like this:

public interface INameAddress extends IName, IAddress {}

public class Person implements INameAddress {

✂

   // class definition here

✂

}

public class Passenger implements INameAddress {

✂

   // class definition here

✂

}

Now bring agent into the picture (Figure 3-16).

In Java, it looks like this:

public class Person implements INameAddress {

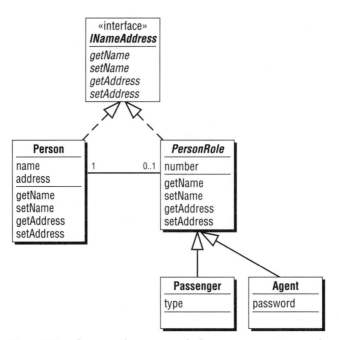

Figure 3-16.   A person is composed of one or more person roles; a person role specializes into different kinds of person roles.

```
✂
        // class definition here
✂
}

public abstract class PersonRole implements INameAddress {
✂
        // class definition here
✂
}

public class Passenger extends PersonRole {
✂
        // class definition here
✂
}

public class Agent extends PersonRole {
✂
```

```
            // class definition here
✂
}
```

Now consider a NameAddressUI object.

It's a user interface (UI) object, one that contains a number of smaller, handcrafted or GUI–builder-generated UI objects: text fields, buttons, scrollable lists, and the like.

In addition, and more importantly (from an object-modeling perspective), a NameAddressUI object knows some number of objects in classes that implement the INameAddress interface.

The real power is that the NameAddressUI is not hardwired to objects in just one class. Instead, it works with objects from any class that implements the INameAddress interface (Figure 3-17).

In Java, it looks like this:

```
public class NameAddressUI {
✂
    // attribute / private / association
    private Vector nameAddresses = new Vector();

    // method / public / accessor for object association values
    public void addNameAddress(INameAddress aNameAddress) {
        // only add objects of the type INameAddress to the vector
        this.nameAddresses.addElement(aNameAddress) ; }
✂
}
```

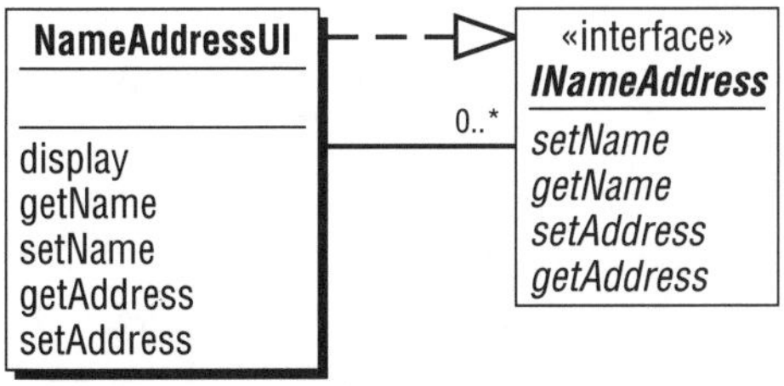

Figure 3-17. Each name-address UI object is composed of a collection of INameAddress objects.

Impact: interfaces change the very nature of an association, of one object knowing other objects. As an object, one's perspective shifts from, "I hold a collection of sale objects" to "I hold a collection of ISell objects," meaning, objects in *any* class that implements the ISell interface. Intriguing!

Here a UI object holds a collection of objects from any class that implements a specific interface. This shifts an object-model builder's attention to "what interface does that object need to provide?" rather than "what class(es) of objects should I limit myself to?"

With interfaces an object model gains better abstraction and simpler results. The implementation also benefits from this simplification.

Now, take a look at the corresponding scenario (Figure 3-18).

Additional impact: interfaces change the heart and soul of working out dynamics with scenarios. A scenario is a time-ordered sequence of object interactions. Now, as an object in a scenario, one's perspective shifts from, "I send a message to a sale object" to "I send a message to an ISell object," meaning, an object in *any* class that implements the ISell interface. Doubly intriguing!

In this scenario, a UI object sends a message to any object in a class that implements the needed interface. For the receiving object, it no longer matters where its class is in the class hierarchy, and it no longer matters if its class spells out a different implementation (time vs. size tradeoffs will always be with us).

With interfaces, your attention shifts from "what class of objects am I working with now?" to "what's the interface and what's the interface that I need from whatever kind of object I might work with, now or in the future?"

With interfaces, you spend more time thinking about the interfaces that you need, rather than who might implement that interface.

With interfaces, each scenario delivers more impact. Redundancy across related scenarios goes down.

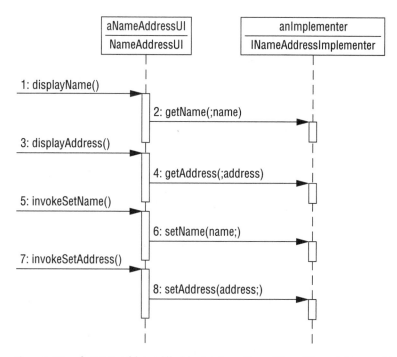

Figure 3-18. A name-address UI object, interacting with an INameAddress object.

What's the impact of interfaces? Reuse within the current app and greater likelihood of reuse in future apps. In addition, you gain simplified (easier to develop and maintain) models that are flexible, extensible, and support pluggability.

This is a nice outcome for relatively modest effort.

3.3.3   Factor Out for Analogous Apps

Factor Out for Analogous Apps Strategy: *Factor out method signatures that could be applicable in analogous apps. Reason for use: to increase likelihood of using and reusing off-the-shelf classes.*

You can use the "factor out repeaters" strategy to increase the level of abstraction within a class diagram and its scenarios within the problem domain you are currently working.

The "factor out for analogous apps" strategy takes an even broader perspective. You can use this strategy to achieve use and reuse across a family of analogous applications.

Here's how.

3.3.3.1 Categorize to Your Heart's Content

You can categorize business apps in different ways. If inheritance were your only categorization mechanism, you could go absolutely crazy. How could you decide upon just one or just a few ways to categorize what you are working on?

Now you have interfaces. You can use them to categorize classes of objects in multiple ways, across a variety of dimensions.

Consider business apps. Two key (yet certainly not all-inclusive) categories are sales and rentals. In a sales system, some goods are sold for a price. So we could categorize certain classes of objects as being sellable, perhaps reservable, too.

In a rental system, talent, equipment, or space is rented for a date or for an interval of time; the goods are still there, and are rented again and again and again. Here, we could classify certain classes of objects as being rentable, and perhaps reservable, too.

3.3.3.2 Categorize Charlie's Charters Business

How do we categorize Charlie's Charters business? Charlie's Charters is in the rental business: it rents space on a scheduled flight for a specific date.

For a flight description on Charlie's Charters, we can reserve space on a scheduled flight. We can ask it if a seat is available; we can ask it to reserve a seat; and we can ask it to cancel a reservation (Figure 3-19).

Now consider a UI object who knows one or more flight description objects. Without interfaces, it looks like Figure 3-20.

The corresponding scenario is shown in Figure 3-21.

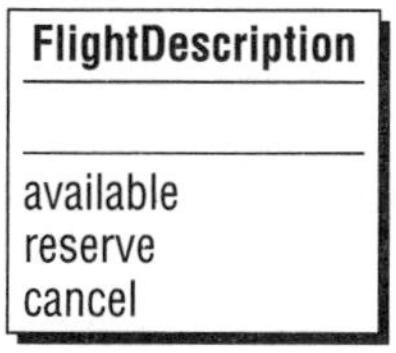

FlightDescription

available
reserve
cancel

Figure 3-19. Methods for reserving space on a scheduled flight.

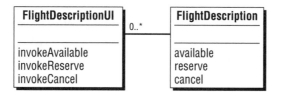

Figure 3-20. A UI class, custom crafted for a flight description.

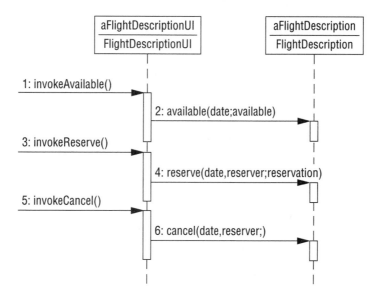

Figure 3-21. UI objects, interacting with objects in just one class (hardwired object interactions).

3.3.3.3 How Can Interfaces Help in This Context?

Charlie's Charters is a no-frills airline. It reserves space on a scheduled flight; it does not reserve specific seat numbers. (Adding SeatMap, Seat, and SeatAssignment classes would take care of that—not a big deal.)

For the Charlie's Charters app, we are interested in reserving space for a given date. We could use an interface called IDateReserve (see Figure 3-22).

We need to add the passenger as a parameter for reserve and cancel. However, since we want this interface to be general, the parameter type should be that of an Object. Let's give it the name "reserver,"—and so we have:

> reserve (date, reserver) and
>
> cancel (date, reserver).

Here is what it looks like in Java:

```
public interface IDateReserve {
    boolean available(Date aDate);
    Object reserve(Date aDate, Object reserver);
    boolean cancel(Date aDate, Object reserver); }
```

Code notes: available and cancel return boolean results. Reserve returns an object, keeping the interface flexible (we aren't needlessly limiting the interface to objects in a specific class or its subclasses). The object that gets that returned object must cast the result into whatever kind of object it expects to get back.

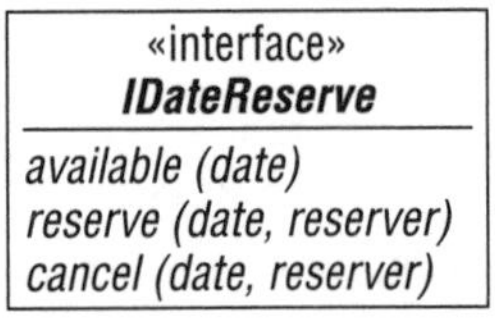

```
«interface»
IDateReserve
─────────────────
available (date)
reserve (date, reserver)
cancel (date, reserver)
```

Figure 3-22.   The IDateReserve interface.

Note that the method signatures are generalized a bit, so they can be applied within any system that has IDateReserve elements within it.

Why bother extracting this analogous interface? Simply put, we are looking for an interface that makes it easy for objects that know how to interact with that interface to "plug in" and make use of that interface. Having off-the-shelf UI components that sport commonly used interfaces saves design, development, and testing time. Very nice indeed.

For example, if you have an object that knows how to interact with an object in any class that implements IDateReserve, then you can use and reuse that object in any app with IDateReserve objects in it. Note that all you care about is the interface; you are free from having to consider the specific class or classes of objects that you might want to interact with. This gives new-found freedom within object-oriented design.

3.3.3.4 An Aside: Some Related Interfaces

A variation on this theme is IDateTimeReserve, which is not needed at Charlie's because a flight description specifies a time of departure. However, if we needed it, it would look like Figure 3-23.

Consider analogous systems such as other rental businesses.

For video rentals, you'd reserve a title for a date (for example, this Saturday). This is another case in which you could use that same IDateReserve interface.

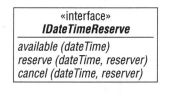

Figure 3-23.   The IDateTimeReserve interface.

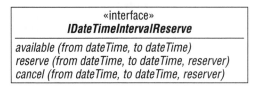

Figure 3-24.   The IDateIntervalReserve interface.

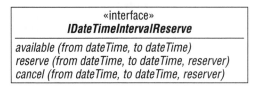

«interface»
IDateTimeIntervalReserve

available (from dateTime, to dateTime)
reserve (from dateTime, to dateTime, reserver)
cancel (from dateTime, to dateTime, reserver)

Figure 3-25.   The IDateTimeIntervalReserve interface.

For hotel rooms, you'd be interested in reserving a certain kind of room (concierge level) for an interval of time (for example, from the fifth to the ninth). You could use an interface called IDateIntervalReserve (Figure 3-24).

For car rentals, you'd reserve a certain kind of car (full-size four-door) for an interval of time (for example, from the fifth at 5 PM until the ninth at 9 PM). You could use an interface called IDateTimeIntervalReserve (Figure 3-25).

3.3.3.5 Using IDateReserve for Charlie's Charters

For Charlie's Charters you need an IDateReserve interface as shown in Figure 3-26.

You can use or reuse any object that knows how to interact with an object in a class that implements the IDateReserve interface.

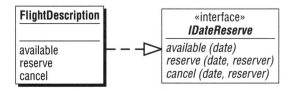

Figure 3-26.   The flight description class implements the IDateReserve interface.

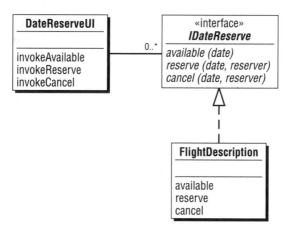

Figure 3-27. UI objects, connected to objects in classes that implement a given interface (flexible associations).

For example, a "date reservation" user interface could interact with an object in any class that implements IDateReserve—a flight reservation object, a video title object, and so on.

With interfaces you get new found flexibility. Now UI objects can connect with an object in any class that implements the correct interface (Figures 3-27 and 3-28).

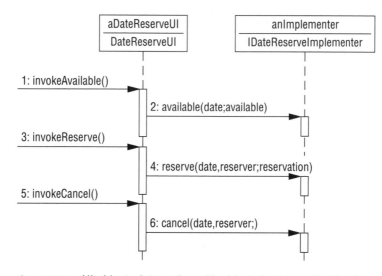

Figure 3-28. UI objects, interacting with objects in classes that implement a given interface (flexible object interactions).

With interfaces, our attention shifts from "what class of objects can I interact with?" to "what's the interface that I can interact with?"

3.3.6.6 Using IDateReserve in Other Apps

Let's consider another date reservation example. Suppose you are designing a system for a temporary help business in which each worker and each piece of equipment is reservable for a date. In this case, a "daily work order" object can interact with any objects in classes that implement the IDateReserve interface (Figures 3-29 and 3-30).

Today, a daily work order might be a collection of workers and pieces of equipment. Next year, it might be a collection of workers, pieces of equipment, and workspace.

What is the impact of change?

Add a new class to your object model: Workspace. Be sure it implements the IDateReserve interface. Connect it with whatever associations it might need (Figure 3-31).

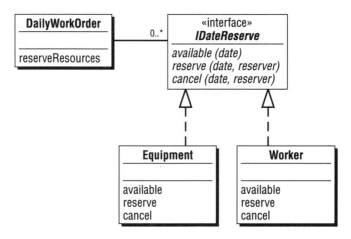

Figure 3-29. Each daily work order object is composed of a collection of IDateReserve objects.

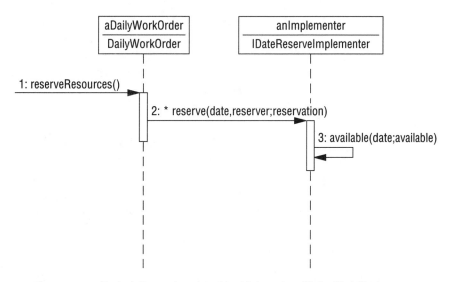

Figure 3-30. Each daily work order object interacts with its IDateReserve objects.

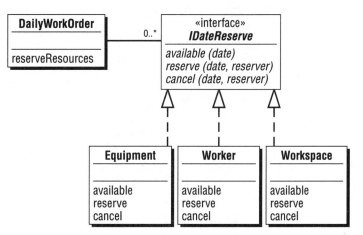

Figure 3-31. Each daily work order object is *still* composed of a collection of IDateReserve objects.

No change to your scenario is needed. The interaction between a daily work order and its IDateReserve objects remains exactly the same.

A daily work order holds a collection of IDateReserve objects. What if it also holds other objects in that collection, objects from classes that don't implement IDateReserve? In this case, a daily work order object can ask an object if it is an instance of IDateReserve. If it is, the daily work order object can then use the interface to interact with that object.*

The point of all this is expandability. By using interfaces, your class diagram and scenarios are organized for change. Instead of being hardwired to a limited number of classes of objects, your design can accommodate objects from present or future classes, just as long as these classes implement the interface(s) that you need.

3.3.4   Factor Out for Future Expansion

Factor Out for Future Expansion Strategy: *Factor out method signatures now, so objects from different classes can be graciously accommodated in the future. Reason for use: to embrace flexibility.*

You can use interfaces as a futurist, too. What if you are wildly successful on your current project? Simply put, the reward for work well done is more work.

So what is next? What other objects might you deal with in the future, objects that could "plug in" more easily, if you could go ahead and establish a suitable interface now?

You can add such interfaces to improve model understanding now and point to change flexibility for the future (hey, this might even get you a pay raise). And you can demonstrate to your customer that your model is ready for expansion—just send more money!

---

*In C++, information about what class an object is in is called run-time type information (RTTI). In Java and Smalltalk, information about what class an object is in is a standard query that can be asked of any object.

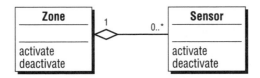

Figure 3-32. A zone and its sensors.

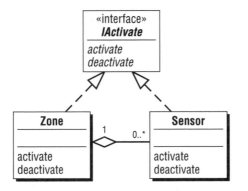

Figure 3-33. Factoring out a common interface.

3.3.4.1 Factoring Out for the Future of Zoe's Zones

Take a look at a zone and its sensors (see Figure 3-32).

Factor out common method signatures into a new interface (see Figure 3-33).

Now adjust the class diagram, so a zone holds a collection of IActi-vate objects (Figure 3-34).

Go even further: an IActivate object consists of other IActivates (Figure 3-35).

However, this is going a bit too far. An IActivate is an interface; it has no attributes, it has no associations. So showing an association with a constraint on an interface really is going a bit too far. You cannot re-quire an interface to implement an association.

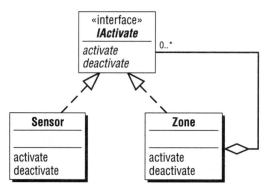

Figure 3-34.   A zone and its collection of IActivates.

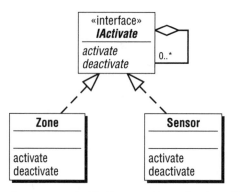

Figure 3-35.   An IActivate and its collection of IActivates (too far).

Now, what you *can* do is use method naming conventions that imply attributes and methods:

- get/set method signatures imply attributes

   getStatus and setStatus

- add/remove method signatures imply associations

   addIActivate and removeIActivate.

By using the add/remove naming convention, we end up with a new, improved IActivate interface (Figure 3-36).

Figure 3-37 depicts a corresponding scenario, showing add, activate, and deactivate. Zone is an example of an IActivateGroupImplementer, Sensor is an example of an IActivateImplementer.

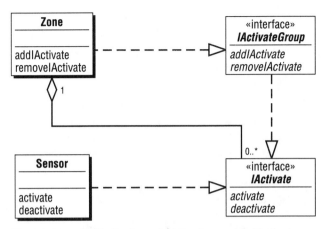

Figure 3-36. An IActivate and adding/removing IActivates.

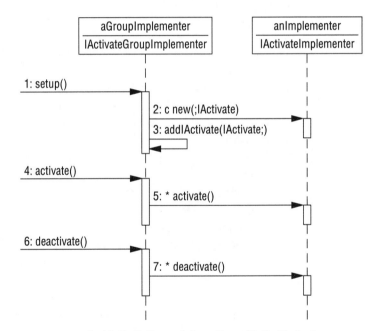

Figure 3-37. An IActivateGroup interacting with its IActivates.

In Java, it looks like this:

```
public interface IActivate {
    void activate();
    void deactivate(); }
```

```java
public interface IActivateGroup extends IActivate {
    void addIActivate(IActivate anIActivate);
    void removeIActivate(IActivate anIActivate); }

public class Sensor implements IActivate {
✂

    // methods / public / IActivate implementation
    public void activate() { /* code goes here */ }
    public void deactivate() { /* code goes here */ }
✂
}


public class Zone implements IActivateGroup {
✂

    // attributes / private / associations
    private Vector activates = new Vector();

    // methods / public / IActivateGroup implementation
    public addIActivate(IActivate anIActivate) {
        this.activates.addElement(anIActivate); }
    public removeIActivate(IActivate anIActivate) {
        this.activates.removeElement(anIActivate); }
    public void activate() {
        // iterate through the vector of "IActivates" and ask each one to
        // activate itself
        Enumeration activateList = this.activates.elements();
        while (activateList.hasMoreElements()) {
            // must cast the element to IActivate
            IActivate anIActivate = (IActivate)activateList.nextElement();
            anIActivate.activate(); }
    }
    public void deactivate() {
        // iterate through the vector of "IActivates" and ask each one to
        // deactivate itself
        Enumeration activateList = this.activates.elements();
        while (activateList.hasMoreElements()) {
            // must cast the element to IActivate
            IActivate anIActivate = (IActivate)activateList.nextElement();
            anIActivate.deactivate(); }
    }
✂
}
```

3.3.4.2 Flexibility, Extensibility, and Pluggability for Zoe's Zones

One aspect of flexibility, extensibility, and pluggability is being able to combine objects that you are already working with in new ways—combinations that you might not have anticipated at first.

Now a zone could be a collection of other zones, which could be a collection of sensors. And a sensor could be a collection of other sensors. Nice.

A sensor could be a collection of zones, but this would probably not make much sense. Interfaces allow you to express what kind of behavior must be supported. However, reasonableness applies when it comes to deciding what to plug together!

Another aspect of extensibility is being able to add in new classes of objects: ones that you can anticipate now, and ones that may surprise you in the future.

Look at the interfaces that you are establishing and consider what other classes of objects might implement that same interface at some point in the future.

For zones and sensors, you might look ahead to additional IActivates: switches, motors, conveyor belts, and robot arms (Figure 3-38).

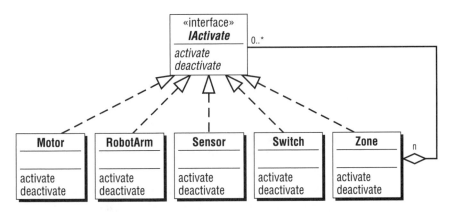

Figure 3-38. Adding in some new IActivates—flexibility, extensibility, pluggability.

When the time comes, you could simply add the new classes, new interface implementers, to the class diagram.

The scenario stays exactly the same as before, up to the point of sending a message to an interface implementer.

3.4   A Short Interlude: Where to Add Interfaces

Okay, so at this point, you might be beginning to wonder about when and where to use an interface. After all, for a fully flexible design, you could include interfaces *everywhere:*

- An interface for every method signature, separating signature from implementation

- An interface for every method signature

- An interface at each end of an association, so each end of the association is not hard-wired to objects in just one class

- An interface for every method call, so you can plug in an alternative implementation of that method any time you choose to.

Very flexible? Yes. Very unwieldy? Yes—and that is the problem. If you set off to build the most flexible software in the universe, you will most definitely run out of time, budget, and resources before you get there. "As flexible as possible" is not a reasonable design objective.

So where does it make sense to add in an interface? Where should you invest in designing-in flexibility? Here is a strategy on this very matter:

Where to Add Interfaces Strategy: Add interfaces at those points in your design that you anticipate change: (1) Connect with an interface implementer rather than with an object in a specific class; (2) Send a message to an interface implementer rather than to an object in a specific class; and (3) Invoke a plug-in method rather than a method defined within a class.

Figure 3-39.   Interfaces let you specify the plug-in points, the points of flexibility, within your design.

You've already seen the first two parts of this strategy; the third part is coming up later in this chapter.

There's a picture of this strategy in our minds that needs to somehow get in print. The next four figures visually express this strategy.

When you add an interface, you are adding in a plug-in point, a place where you can plug-in any object from any class that implements the interface (Figure 3-39). Think of an interface as a plug-in point, like a socket on a circuit board.

Rather than connect with objects in a specific class, you can connect with objects in any class that implements an interface (Figure 3-40). One might put it this way: The association connects to a plug-in point.

Rather than send a message to an object in a specific class, you can send a message to an interface implementer (Figure 3-41). Then you can plug in to that plug-in point absolutely any object from any class that implements that interface. You get added flexibility, at the points where you need it (or anticipate that you need it).

Sometimes you might need to vary the implementation of a method. That is to say, you need the ability to unplug one algorithm

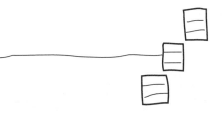

Figure 3-40.   Connect with an interface implementer not limited to just objects in a single class.

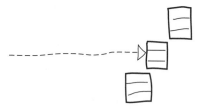

Figure 3-41. Send a message to an interface implementer not limited to just objects in a single class.

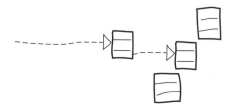

Figure 3-42. Delegate to an interface implementer so you won't be restricted to the methods defined in just one class.

and plug-in another one (Figure 3-42). We are not suggesting general-purpose function blobs or master controllers here (we get a wee bit queasy whenever we see a class name ending with the suffix –er). Yet there are times where a plug-in point for some pluggable behavior brings some algorithmic flexibility that we've found quite helpful.

Where should you add interfaces? Add interfaces to those places where you, as a designer, see the cost-justified need for association flexibility, messaging flexibility, and algorithmic flexibility.

Having completed this short interlude, let's continue with more strategies for interface-centric design.

3.5   Design-in Interfaces

The previous section presented four strategies on how to *factor out* interfaces, that is to say, extract out interfaces from an evolving object model. And factoring-out seems like a good way to begin working with interfaces. Indeed, that's how we got started.

Yet a better approach is to *design in* interfaces in the first place. In other words, look for and establish interfaces all along the way, right as you build your object model. Then, as a crosscheck, you can use the factoring-out strategies to check your interface design and to find additional opportunities for adding flexibility using composition and interfaces.

This two-pass approach—design in and then factor out—mirrors what we've done in practice, the discovery process we've gone through on a variety of projects.

Keep in mind why you design with interfaces. It's all about *substitution,* being able to substitute an object in one class for an object in another class. In fact, each interface within a design embodies two kinds of substitution: plug-in substitution or interaction substitution.

Plug-in substitution means that you can interchangeably put in any object that implements the required interface.

Interaction substitution means that you can send messages to an object in one class as if it were an object in some other class. (Inheritance is one way to do this; yet interfaces let you do this even when the classes you are working with are not directly related via inheritance.) The receiving object might do the work itself, or it might ask another object to do the real work for you (delegation). Either way, the work gets done.

Here is a list of the design-in strategies:

- Design-in interfaces based on common features
- Design-in interfaces based on role doubles
- Design-in interfaces based on behavior across roles
- Design-in interfaces based on collections and members
- Design-in interfaces based on common interactions
- Design-in interfaces based on intra-class roles
- Design-in interfaces based on a need for plug-in algorithms
- Design-in interfaces based on a need for plug-in feature sequences

Let's consider and apply these strategies one by one—and then in combination with one another.

3.5.1   Design-in Interfaces Based on Common Features

As soon as you first write up a features list, you can identify important interfaces for your model. Here's what it takes:

Design-In, from Features to Interfaces Strategy:

1. *Look for a common feature, one you need to provide in different contexts.*

2. *Identify a set of method names that correspond to that feature.*

3. *Add an interface.*

4. *Identify implementers.*

It's time for an example—this time from Larry's Loans. Larry and his fellow loan sharks are very interested in both loan applicants and borrowers (loan-account holders).

Consider this excerpt from Larry's features list:

1. Total outstanding balances for a borrower

2. Total outstanding balances for an applicant (may or may not be a borrower)

3. List accounts and limits for a borrower (a limit is the maximum amount one can borrow, as in a credit-card limit)

4. List accounts and limits for an applicant (may or may not be a borrower)

Jot down some common method names:

totalBorrowingBalance

listAccountsAndLimits

Now define some interfaces.

If you planned using either name in any context, you could define three interfaces: one for one method signature, one for the other method signature, and one as a combination of the other two interfaces. If you did this with every interface, though, you'd end up with a needless explosion in the number of interfaces in your design. Flexible, yet not simple.

At the other extreme, if these two method names were so closely related that you'd always want them implemented in tandem, then you could say it all in one interface. Simple, not needlessly flexible.

So consider the middle ground between these two extremes. In this case, choose the middle ground: "total" in many contexts, "list and total" in other contexts (Figure 3-43).

In Java syntax, it's:

```
public interface ITotalBorrowingBalance {
    BigDecimal totalBorrowingBalance();
}
public interface IAccount extends ITotalBorrowingBalance {
    Enumeration listAccountsAndLimits();
}
```

Next, build a class diagram around those interfaces. Loan applicant and borrower can implement a common interface. Borrower will do the real work; a loan applicant will delegate its work to its corresponding borrower (Figure 3-44).

Note that Borrower defines the real work to be done; each loan applicant simply sends a message to its corresponding borrower

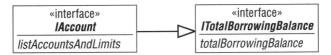

Figure 3-43. Feature-inspired interfaces.

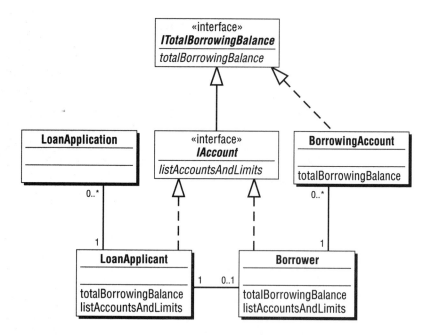

Figure 3-44. From features to an interface to a class diagram.

object, letting it do all the work (delegation at work once again). See Figure 3-45.

Now you can take any loan applicant or any borrower and ask the same question: what is your loan–borrowing balance? So problem-domain containers (like bank) and user-interface objects (like loan-balance lists) can readily work with objects from either class in exactly the same way.

Going from features to interfaces gives you a way to:

- categorize similar functionality.

  Similar in name, with the potential for some behind-the-scenes delegation

- explicitly represent those categorizations.

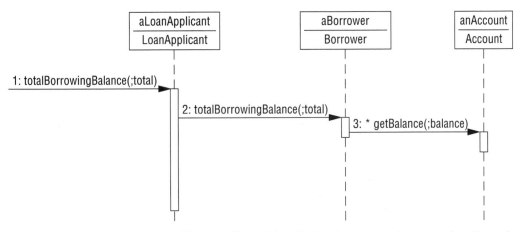

Figure 3-45. A loan applicant delegates to a borrower; a borrower does the real work.

3.5.2 Design-in Interfaces Based on Role Doubles

For each role in your model, you can name an interface in its honor and then let other roles offer that same interface. All of the others will delegate the real work back to the original role-player.

The strategy looks like this:

Design-in, from Role Doubles to Interfaces Strategy:

1. *Take a role and turn its method signatures into a role-inspired interface.*

2. *Let another role (a "role double") offer that same interface by:*

   - *implementing that interface, and*

   - *delegating the real work back to the original role player.*

Larry's Loans is most especially interested in borrowers. For Larry and his cohorts, borrower is the most important role (after all, their business and profits come from their borrowers). For a given borrower, Larry needs to see the total approved lending limits and a listing of the lending limits available to that borrower.

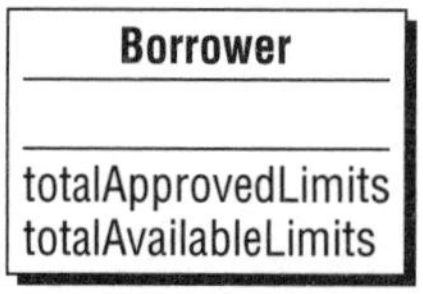

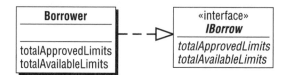

Figure 3-46.   Begin with a role.

Figure 3-47.   An interface corresponding to a role.

First, select a role. The borrower role looks something like Figure 3-46.

Next, add a role-inspired interface (Figure 3-47).

Finally, let another role implement that interface, delegating the real work back to the original role player (Figure 3-48).

Composition and interfaces work hand-in-hand. A loan applicant may play the role of a borrower (composition). Both loan applicant and borrower provide the same interface.

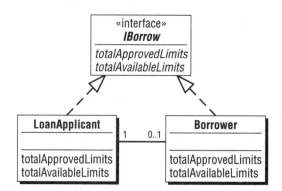

Figure 3-48.   Role doubles.

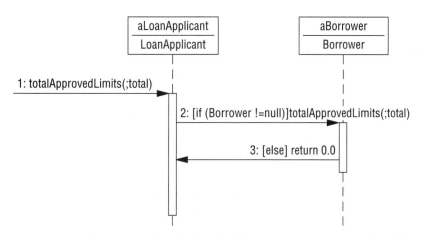

Figure 3-49. Ask a loan-applicant object; it delegates to its borrower object (If it has one).

Actually, the model indicates that a loan applicant *might* play the role of a borrower. If someone asks a loan-applicant object to "total its approved limits" when it has no corresponding borrower object, the loan-applicant object simply returns zero (and avoids messaging a borrower altogether).

Figure 3-49 shows how a loan-applicant delegates to its borrower.

Expressed in Java, IBorrow, Borrower, and LoanApplicant look like this:

```
public interface IBorrow {
    BigDecimal totalApprovedLimits();
    BigDecimal totalAvailableLimits();
}
public Borrower implements IBorrow {
✀
    public BigDecimal totalApprovedLimits() {/*real work*/}
    public BigDecimal totalAvailableLimits() {/*real work*/}
✀
}
```

```
public LoanApplicant implements IBorrow {

    private Borrower borrower; /*add/remove with add/remove methods*/
    public BigDecimal totalApprovedLimits() {
        if (this.borrower != null)
            return this.borrower.totalApprovedLimits(); /*delegate*/
        else return (new BigDecimal (0.0));
    }
    public BigDecimal totalAvailableLimits() {
        if (this.borrower != null)
            return this.borrower.totalAvailableLimits(); /*delegate*/
        else return (new BigDecimal (0.0));
    }

}
```

Interfaces give you a way to treat an object in one class just as if it were an object in some other class. And that's a good thing; it allows you to focus on time-ordered sequences of object interactions that are more important, more revealing, more able to help you improve the model you are working on.

3.5.3 Design-in Interfaces Based on Behavior Across Roles

Another place to design-in interfaces is to look at a party and consider what it does across its collection of party roles.

The same principle applies to a place (for example, an airport) and its roles (day operations, night operations); it also applies to a thing (an aircraft) and its roles (military or civilian).

3.5.3.1 Should a Party Support Role-at-a-Time Interfaces?

Back to the party for now. A party has a collection of party roles. Should the party itself offer single-role interfaces (Figure 3-50)?

If so, then a party could delegate to its loan applicant and the loan applicant could delegate to its borrower (Figure 3-51).

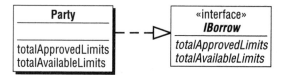

Figure 3-50. Should party offer single-role interfaces?

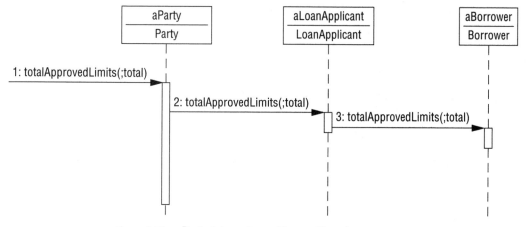

Figure 3-51. Party interacting with specific roles.

Yet why ask a party questions that apply to just a role? You don't need to. Instead, in scenarios, you end up interacting directly with a borrower object or a loan applicant object.

Hence, should you add an IBorrow interface to a party? No way. Why? Adding that interface needlessly complicates a party; you just don't need it.

Again, don't add single-role-specific interfaces to a party (this would make party too complicated, especially enterprise-wide); for single-role-specific interaction, let the party interact with the role's methods itself, rather than through a separately defined interface.

So when might you add a role-related interface to a party? Ever?

3.5.3.2 Should a Party Support "Behavior Across Roles" Interfaces?

Consider this: What does a party object do best? Simply put, it enforces behavior across its many roles.

Let's explore this a bit further.

A party might have a number of roles. Here, a party can have two roles; one of those roles might have a subsequent role (see Figure 3-52).

In general, a party might have many roles (loan applicant, borrower, shareholder, lender, manager, executive, and so on). To support a party's need to interact across its collection of roles, each role could implement a common role interface. In this case, that common role interface is IAuthorize (see Figure 3-53).

Note the designed-in flexibility: it's easy to drop in a new role, as long as that role implements the common interface(s) for party to iterate over. Party does what party does best: enforce business rules that apply across its roles.

Should a party support "behavior across roles" interfaces? Yes!

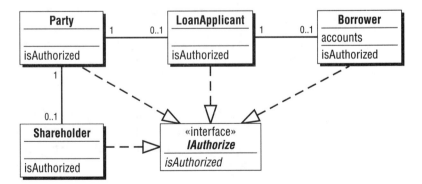

Figure 3-52.   An interface for behavior across roles.

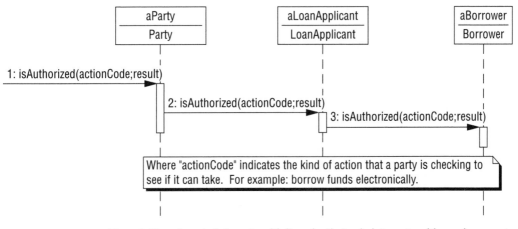

Figure 3-53.   A party interacts with its role; that role interacts with a subsequent role.

3.5.4   Design-in Interfaces Based on Collections and Members

With each class you add to your model, you can add depth by considering what interfaces it needs for it to do its job as a collection itself, and then as a member within some other collection. Here's how:

Design-in, from Collections and Members to Interfaces Strategy:

1. *Does your object hold a collection of other objects? If so:*

   a. *Consider the potential "across the collection" method signatures.*

   b. *If other collections might offer the same set of method signatures, then design in that common interface.*

2. *Is your object a member within a collection? If so:*

   If that object needs to provide an interface similar to the collections it is in, then design in that common interface.

3. *Identify implementers.*

> «interface»
> ***ITotalApprovedLimit***
> *totalApprovedLimit*

Figure 3-54.   A collection-inspired interface (i).

To begin with, does your object hold a collection of other objects? Collections are just about everywhere:

- If it's a party (person or organization), it has a collection of roles.

- If it's a role, it has a collection of moments or intervals.

- If it's a place or container, it has a collection of moments or intervals.

- If it's a moment or interval, it might have a collection of subsequent moments or intervals.

- If it's an item description, it might have a collection of corresponding specific items (actual things to keep track of).

- If it's an item description, it might have a collection of even more detailed item descriptions.

For an example, consider Larry's Loans.

An application is a collection of approvals; each approval sets an approved limit (one that might be more, less, or the same as the amount originally applied for).

As a collection, we could ask an application to total its approved limits. That's a generally useful interface (See Figure 3-54).

As a member in a collection, we could ask an object to compare its approved amount vs. the applied-for amount. An approval object would have to interact with its corresponding application object to work out the answer. That's another interesting addition to the interface we are working on (See Figure 3-55).

The corresponding class diagram looks like Figure 3-56.

«interface»
ICompareAppliedVsApproved
compareAppliedVsApproved

Figure 3-55. A collection-inspired interface (ii).

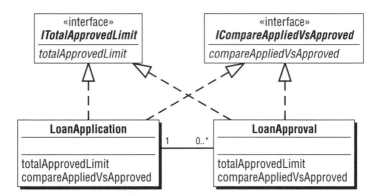

Figure 3-56. From a collection itself and a collection member: first to an interface, and then to a class diagram.

And the corresponding scenario looks like Figure 3-57.

The collection-inspired interface is ITotalApprovedLimit. Ask a loan application for its total approved limits and it interacts with each of its corresponding approval objects, returning the total approved limit. Ask a loan approval for its total approved limits and it simply returns its own approved amount.

In fact, you could plug in an object in any class that implements this interface in either column of the scenario.

Note this added twist. If you plug something into the left position, though, the interactions that follow might be different. It might, for example, implement its own "total approved limit" method and return the result to the sender. Or it might interact with some number of other objects, not shown in the scenario.

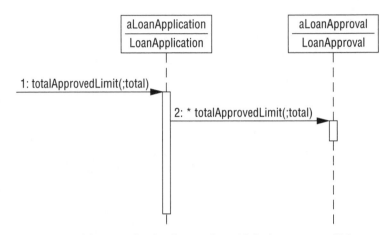

Figure 3-57. A loan application interacting with its loan approval(s).

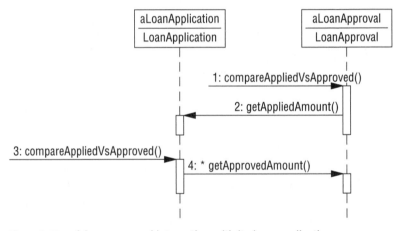

Figure 3-58. A loan approval interacting with its loan application.

On the other hand, take a look at the member-in-a-collection-inspired interface, ICompareAppliedVsApproved (Figure 3-58).

Note the two paths. Ask a loan approval object to compare applied vs. approved; it interacts with its one loan application, makes a comparison, and returns the result to you. Or ask a loan application object to compare applied vs. approved; it interacts with each of its loan approvals, totals the approved amounts, makes a comparison, and returns the result to you.

Examining collections and members gives you a way to establish common interfaces for both a collection and its members (first from a collection's perspective and then from a member's perspective). With the same interface, you end up with broader answers from a collection and more specific answers from a member. This brings more meaningful content to the model sooner, as well as provides a useful abstraction for thinking about and working with that added content.

3.5.5   Design-in Interfaces Based on Common Interactions

When working out dynamics with scenarios, you might come across similar interactions going on between one column and others (Figure 3-59).

When you see similar interactions, it's a good time to design in an interface. Why? To raise the abstraction level within your model. To explicitly capture the interaction commonality. To make the scenario "pluggable" (so you can unplug one interface implementer and plug in another one).

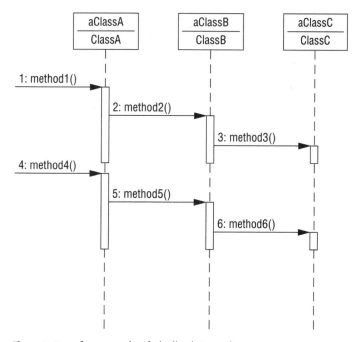

Figure 3-59.   An example of similar interactions.

Here's the strategy:

Design-in, from Scenarios to Interfaces Strategy:

1. *Look for similar interactions.*

2. *Add an interface-implementer column.*

    Use this naming convention:

    I<what it does> Implementer.

3. *Add an interface: I<what it does>.*

4. *Identify implementers.*

Back to Larry's Loans we go, this time beginning with a scenario for assessing profit and risk, the two key aspects of any financial deal. For a loan applicant, we can assess risk. For a borrower, someone who has borrowed money from Larry's Loans, we can assess both profit and risk. The scenario looks like Figure 3-60.

Look at the similar interactions. The strongest similarity is in the assess-risk scenario. A loan applicant asks each of its applications to assess the risk it poses; then a loan applicant asks its corresponding borrower object to assess its risk.

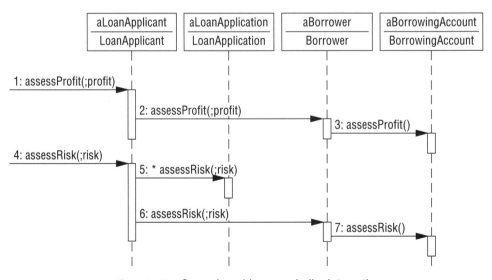

Figure 3-60.   Scenarios with some similar interactions.

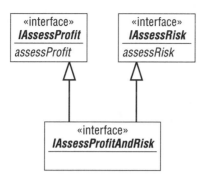

Figure 3-61.   A scenario-inspired interface.

Another similarity in interaction occurs when a loan applicant asks a borrower to assess its risk or to assess its profit.

So take the opportunity to introduce new interfaces (Figure 3-61).

But wait. If assessing profit *always* has assessing risk as a companion (and it always does, in real life), then we really don't need an IAssess interface after all. Here's why:

Interface Granularity Strategy: *If a method signature can only exist with others, then add it directly to an interface definition with those others (no need for a separate, one-signature interface).*

You can use that strategy to keep your number of interfaces down to a more modest level, as in Figure 3-62.

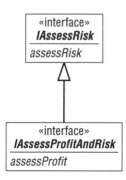

Figure 3-62.   Interfaces, upon applying the "interface granularity" strategy.

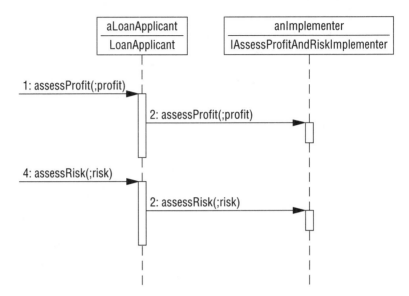

Figure 3-63. Scenarios with an interface implementer.

Okay, with the interfaces established, simplify the scenario itself. How? Use a single "interface implementer" column to represent the implementers of that interface: application, borrower, and borrowing account (Figure 3-63).

Taking these new interfaces into a class diagram, you get Figure 3-64.

So what does this mean? It means that:

- You can ask a borrower object to assess its risk. It does so by interacting with its borrowing account objects.

- You can ask an application object to assess its risk. It does so by interacting with whatever objects it knows (for example, credit reports).

- You can ask a loan-applicant object to assess its risk. It does so by interacting with its application objects and its borrower object.

Working from scenarios to interfaces gives you a way to classify objects with similar functionality and interactions, regardless of what classes those objects might be in, now or in the future.

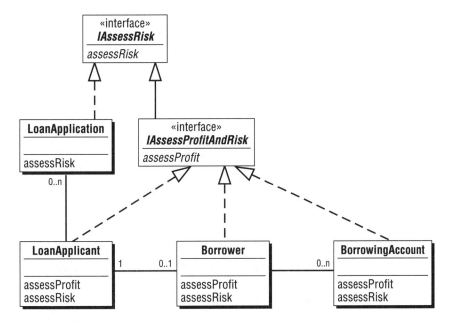

Figure 3-64. From scenarios to interfaces to a class diagram.

3.5.6 Design-in Interfaces Based on Intra-class Roles

Objects rarely do anything interesting by themselves. Most often, an object interacts with objects in other classes to get something done.

Yet sometimes objects within a class interact with other objects in that same class. How can you recognize when this is the case? Take the time to consider each class and the roles the objects in that class might play, interacting with other objects in that same class.

Design-in, from Intra-Class Roles to Interfaces Strategy:

1. *Identify roles that objects within a class can play.*

2. *Establish an interface for each of those roles.*

3. *Identify implementers.*

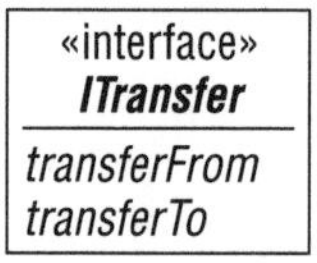

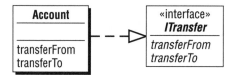

Figure 3-65.   An interface inspired by examining intra-class roles.

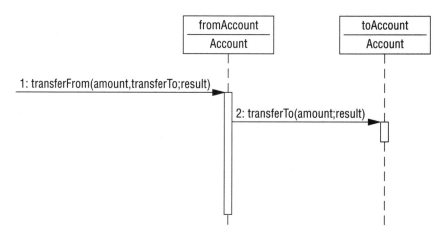

Figure 3-66.   From intra-class roles to interfaces to class diagram.

At Larry's Loans, there are accounts. In an account transfer, one account acts as an origin ("transfer from") and another account acts as a destination ("transfer to").

Examining intra-class roles leads us to the interface in Figure 3-65.

So the Account class gets some added depth to it, as the implementer of the interface (Figure 3-66).

We end up with a scenario with interactions between two objects in the same class: a "transfer from" object and a "transfer to" object (Figure 3-67).

Figure 3-67.   Objects in the same class interacting with each other.

This strategy uses interfaces in yet another way: this time, to abstract up major interaction categories when objects in the same class interact with each other in some collaborative way—and to explicitly model those interaction categories in a class diagram.

3.5.7 Design-in Interfaces Based on a Need for Plug-in Algorithms

When it comes to building better object models, once the overall model shape is in place, methods are where the action is, where strategic advantage comes into play.

An object model without methods is not very exciting. All you end up with is a well-structured data-holding system. An object model that is feature-rich and correspondingly method-rich represents strategic advantage, genuine business advantage in the global marketplace.

In a class, you define a method that applies to each object in that class. It's something that each object can do itself. Yes, there is some potential for variation in what that method does (based upon the state of that object and interactions with related objects), yet the algorithm for each variation is set.

What happens when you require far more algorithmic diversity for objects within a single class? When you find you need algorithmic flexibility, use an interface and some plug-in algorithms—a specific usage context for what is sometimes referred to as a strategy pattern [Gamma 95]. Here is the strategy:

When to Use Plug-in Algorithms and Interfaces Strategy: *Use a plug-in algorithm and interface when you find this combination of problems:*

- *An algorithm you want to use can vary from object to object within a single class*

- *An algorithm is complex enough that you cannot drive its variation using attribute values alone.*

- *An algorithm is different for different categories of objects within a class—and even within those categories (hence, adding a category-description class won't resolve this problem).*

- *An algorithm you want to use will be different over time and you don't know at this point what all those differences will be.*

When this happens, you can design-in an interface so you can plug-in the functionality you need, on an object-by-object basis.

Here is the strategy:

Design-in, from Plug-in Algorithms to Interfaces Strategy:

1. *Look for useful functionality you'd like to "plug in."*
2. *Add a plug-in point, using an interface.*
3. *Identify implementers.*

At Larry's Loans, we need a way to validate the terms of a borrowing account. Terms include restrictions on interest rate, compounding method, and prepayment penalties. And yet validating:

- is different for different kinds of terms.
- is different even for the same kind of term (so adding a "term category description" class won't help us here).
- is going to change over time, in ways we don't know in advance.

So begin tackling these problems by adding an interface (see Figure 3-68).

Now add the plug-in point in a class diagram (see Figure 3-69).

```
«interface»
IValidateTerm
validateTerm
```

Figure 3-68. A plug-in inspired interface.

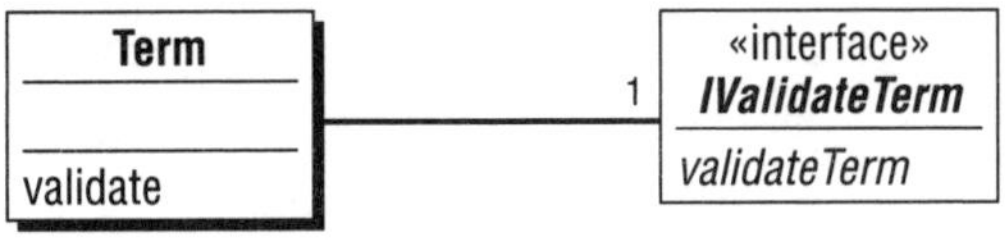

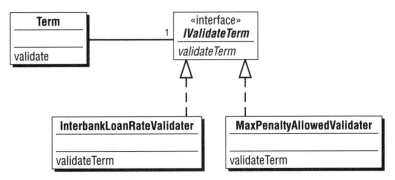

Figure 3-69. Adding a plug-in point.

Figure 3-70. Adding something to plug-in at the plug-in point.

Next, take it a step further, adding something to actually plug into that plug-in point (see Figure 3-70).

An IValidateTerm object is an algorithm you can plug into a term object. For one term you might want to plug in an algorithm that compares the interest rate being charged with the interbank loan rate. For another term, you might want to plug in an algorithm that compares the penalty stated in that term with the maximum allowed by law within the applicable geopolitical region. And so on.

So you create a term object; create the appropriate validater; plug the validater into the term object; and you're ready to go.

The "validate a term" scenario looks like Figure 3-71.

Note that the term itself is passed along to the validater, so the implementer can in turn send messages to the term object, to get whatever the implementer needs to do its job (this kind of interaction is sometimes referred to as a "callback").

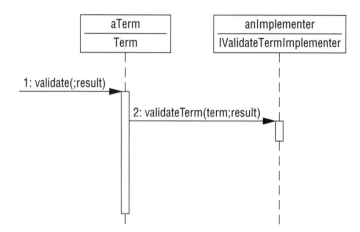

Figure 3-71.   Delegating to a plug-in point.

Here's how to express it in Java:

```
public interface IValidateTerm {
    int validateTerm(Term term);
}
public class Term {

    private IValidateTerm validater;
    public void addValidater (IValidateTerm validater) {
            this.validater = validater; }
    public int validate() {
        return this.validater.validateTerm(this); }

}
```

So what might happen when you plug in a specific term validater? It depends on the behavior of what you plug in, of course. Figure 3-72 is an example.

Designing-in interfaces at plug-in points gives you a way to design for current or anticipated algorithmic diversity for objects within a class, adding algorithmic flexibility to your design.

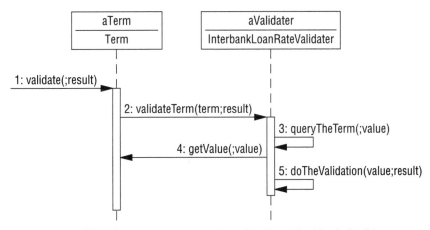

Figure 3-72. What happens once you ask a plug-in method to do its thing depends on that plug-in method.

3.5.8 Design-in Interfaces Based on a Need for Plug-in Feature Sequences

But first, it's time for another short interlude about designing with designs (plural). Plugging in feature sequences is another good reason for systematically designing interfaces.

3.5.8.1 Short Interlude: Effective Design Requires Designs

Design is all about making comparisons, tradeoffs, and judgments.

It's good engineering practice to develop and consider *several* design alternatives, then assess and select the one you'd like to use for the system under consideration. This occurs (or certainly should occur) again and again and again, throughout the design process.

Strategies and patterns are essential ingredients for assessing and selecting from design alternatives.

Working out dynamics with scenarios is one of the best ways to compare design alternatives.

Sometimes it's important to gather some empirical evidence: Design and build a small part of the system to work out what approach to take on your project.

Please note that this is not an exhortation to look for the *best* design, the one *true* design, or something close (it doesn't exist!). Please also note that you're not reading anything like, "Follow these steps and the very first design you come up with will be the best one." On the other hand, nor are you seeing an endorsement for design by committee—far from it. Good things get accomplished by small groups and even in a small group someone needs to play "chief architect" and make important decisions along the way.

By considering three possibilities, you can look for the best of that set. And nearly always the result will be better than grabbing the first design that pops into your head and running with it.

In fact, good designers often end up with a simpler overall result, with a sense of "Gee, that was obvious" or "I'm glad we got there, but it would have been nice to get there sooner." Such is the nature of good design. Yes, strategies and patterns get you there sooner. Yet this "collapsing of complexity" and "aha!" insight are an integral part of designing for even the very best software designers.

The best design work we do occurs with teams of about 10 designers. We routinely design in three parallel subteams. After 30 minutes of design, each sub-team presents work in progress. We learn from each other. And we come up with a far better design than any one subteam could produce on its own. Sometimes we pick one design out of the three. More often, we merge good ideas from all three. It takes a seasoned mentor to guide the process. A handbook of strategies and patterns is also an essential ingredient.

Now let's try designing with designs.

3.5.8.2 Feature Sequences

Many applications require feature sequences, also known as business events, business activities, or operational procedures. How should you model such sequences?

Consider the following example, adding the feature "make a sale" to Charlie's Charters.

Feature: Make a sale.

Initiate a new sale.

Accept item and quantity.

Accept method of payment.

Accept amount tendered

(make change, record the sale).

Design #1. We could introduce a "feature sequence (FS)" class, as in Figure 3-73.

The first design? Let a make-a-sale object do all the work. It grabs the data values it needs and does everything else. Low encapsulation, low distribution of responsibility, low resiliency to change.

Design #2. Let a make-a-sale object coordinate yet do absolutely no detailed work. It holds collections. It steps through the process of making a sale. It delegates everything it possibly can to the objects it interacts with. It takes care of a transaction's start/commit/abort. It delivers behavior across the collection of objects it knows and interacts with. Moderate encapsulation, moderate distribution of responsibility, and moderate resiliency to change. A reasonable design. Let's try for something even better.

Design #3. Let a problem-domain object do whatever it takes to coordinate making a sale. In other words, let a sale object make a sale (Figure 3-74).

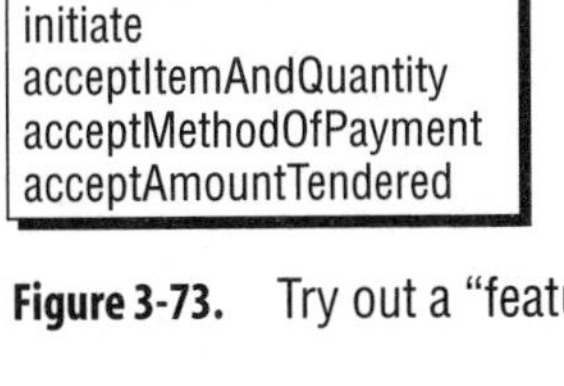

MakeASale_FS
initiate acceptItemAndQuantity acceptMethodOfPayment acceptAmountTendered

Figure 3-73. Try out a "feature sequence"?

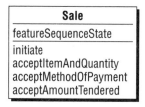

Figure 3-74.   Let a sale coordinate the making of a sale?

High encapsulation, high distribution of responsibility across prob-lem-domain objects, moderate resiliency to change.

Take a closer look at Design #3. How does it work? Consider the scenario in Figure 3-75.

Observation: In this design, human-interaction (HI) objects focus on doing one thing and one thing well: interaction!

Another observation: Rather than thinking of a human-interaction object as a sequence manager, think of it as an **interactive view** of the current states of some problem-domain objects. For example: a store object has a current state; it notifies its listeners (such as a store window object) whenever it changes state; a store window receives such notifications and updates itself accordingly.

Design #4. One more time! Let's take design #3 and improve upon it. The problem with design #3 is that it does not allow you to plug in variations on what it means to make a sale. Plug in? Yes, you can use an interface to define a useful plug-in point—a point in your design where you want to design in added flexibility. (This is another usage context for what is sometimes referred to as a strategy pattern.)

Figure 3-76 shows the Sale class with its corresponding plug-in point for plugging in whatever sequencing is needed to make a sale.

Figure 3-77 shows two implementers of the IMakeASale interface (when you create a sale object, you also "plug in" an object from a class that implements that interface).

Now every time someone asks a sale object to make a sale, that sale object delegates to whatever IMakeASale object it is holding

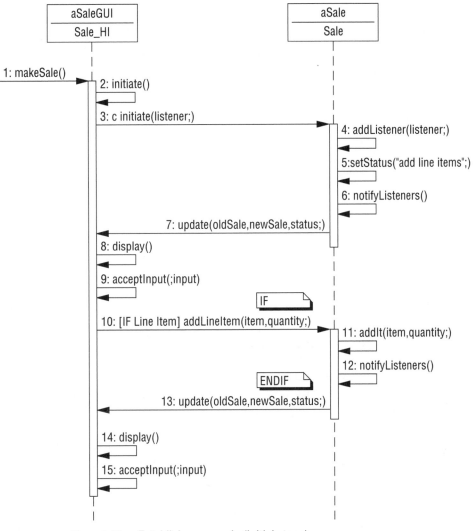

Figure 3-75. Establish a new sale (initial steps).

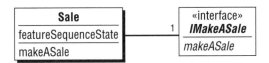

Figure 3-76. A sale with a process plug-in point.

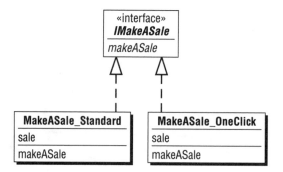

Figure 3-77.   Plug in the process of your choice.

(meaning, whatever object from any class that implements IMakeASale).

Figure 3-78 is an example scenario view.

Note that the sale itself is passed along to the sequencer, so the sequencer can in turn send messages to the sale object, to get whatever the sequencer needs to do its job (another example of a "callback").

For the utmost in flexibility, Design #4 is the winner. It offers high encapsulation, high distribution of responsibility across problem-domain objects, high resiliency to change.

However, it's the winning design of the four designs only if you need such flexibility. Remember it's important to design in flexibility where you need it, not every single place you possibly can!

Wouldn't this fourth design be the obvious first choice for an experienced designer? In practice, we've found the answer to be no. The most flexible design is not always needed. Nor is it intuitively obvious to experienced designers (a team of designers worked on this sequence of designs and only one came up with design #4). Perhaps it's just that as designers we digest so much content that it takes us a while to see what's really needed within a design (as Jerry Weinberg wrote in *Secrets of Consulting,* know-when pays a lot more than know-how). A sense of "collapsing complexity" and "aha!" insight is still very much a part of everyday practice for even very experienced software designers, as it should be.

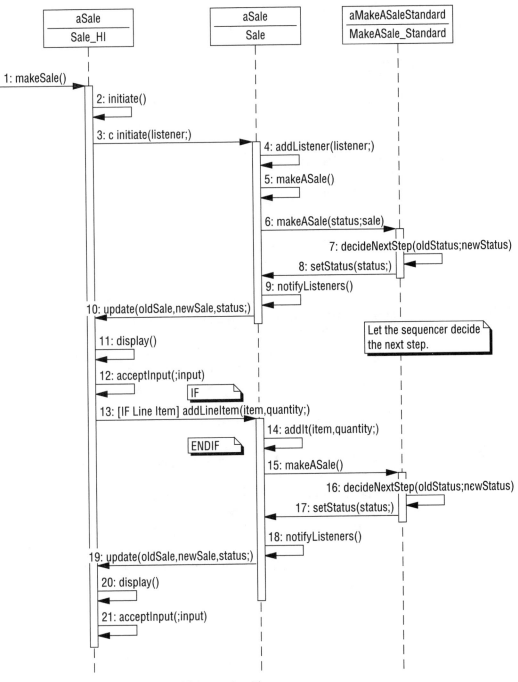

Figure 3-78. Make a sale with a sequencer.

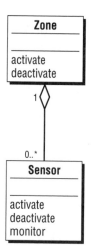

Figure 3-79. A simple yet inflexible diagram: zone and sensor.

3.6   Design with Interfaces: Applying Multiple Strategies

Now apply a number of strategies together, in concert. First apply them for Zoe's Zones. Then apply them for Charlie's Charters.

3.6.1   Designing-in Flexibility Is a Very Good Thing

Begin with a zone and sensor class diagram as in Figure 3-79.

This class diagram is a simple yet inflexible diagram. Why inflexible? Each association is hardwired to objects in a specific class. And each message-send will be hardwired to objects in a specific class.

Design in some flexibility. Review the list of interface strategies:

- Factor-out

    Repeaters

    Proxies

    Analogous apps

    Future expansion

- Design-in

    Common features

    Role doubles
    Behavior across roles

    Collections and members
    Common interactions
    Intra-class roles

    Plug-in algorithms
    Plug-in feature sequences.

Try out the last two in the list.

The monitoring algorithm might vary so greatly from sensor to sensor that we need a plug-in point. Apply the plug-in algorithms strategy.

The overall monitoring sequence for a zone might vary over time. Apply the plug-in feature sequences strategy.

The result looks like Figure 3-80.

Now a zone holds a collection of IActivates—sub-zones, sensors, or anything else that we might want to plug in over time (motors, robot arms, and the like).

And each sensor object gets its own monitoring algorithm. You can plug in the standard default algorithm or develop your own and plug it into the sensor objects you are working with.

Flexibility!

3.6.2 Yet There Usually Is a Design Tradeoff: Simplicity vs. Flexibility

Consider the class diagram in Figure 3-81.

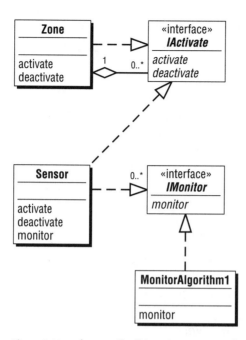

Figure 3-80. A more flexible yet more complex model; flexibility comes with a price.

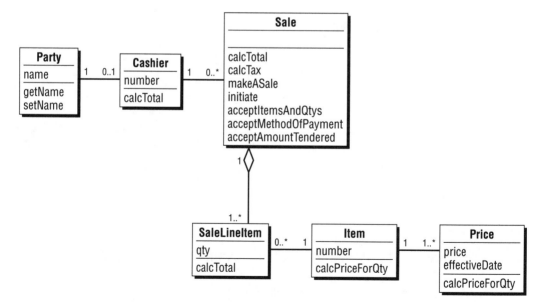

Figure 3-81. A simple class diagram for the retail part of Charlie's business.

This class diagram is simple yet inflexible. Why inflexible? Every association is hard-wired to a specific class. Every message-send will be hard-wired to objects in a specific class. It's simple; it's easy to implement (as long as requirements don't change too drastically along the way).

Now consider a variation on the theme (Figure 3-82).

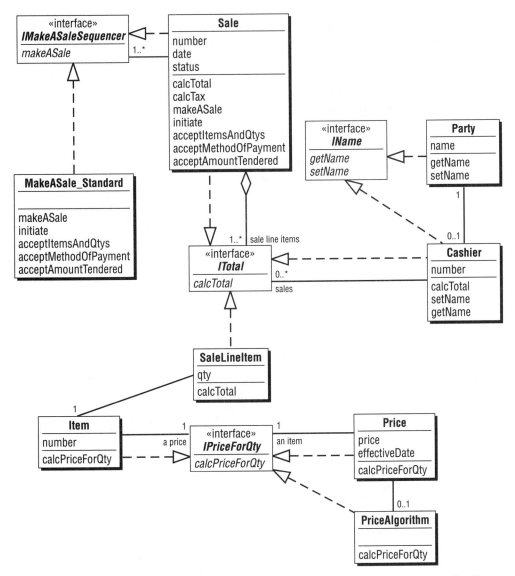

Figure 3-82. A more complicated yet more flexible class diagram for Charlie's business.

This class diagram is more complicated yet more flexible. The diagram includes plug-in points just at those points where the designer anticipates the need to design in some flexibility. A better design? Yes, *if* such flexibility fits within the capability, schedule, and cost constraints for the project at hand.

Add in plug-in points where you need them, where they pay for themselves by adding flexibility in exchange for increased model complexity.

3.7   Naming Interfaces Revisited

With more experience with interfaces in practice, we've thought more and more about what makes a good interface name. We've discovered some more things about useful interface names along the way.

You see, in practice, interface names give you a way to classify:

- The *kinds of classes* whose objects you want to plug into that plug-in point:

  IParty

    getAddress, setAddress

    getLegalName, setLegalName

    getNumber, setNumber

    addPartyRole, getPartyRole, removePartyRole

  with a "kinds of classes" interface name that follows this pattern:

    I<noun, just like a class name>

- Or the *kinds of behavior* you want such objects to exhibit

  ITotal (or ICalcTotal)

    calcTotal

  with a "kinds of behavior" interface name that follows this pattern:

    I<verb, just like a method name>

With these variations on "kinds of behavior:"

- an algorithm plug in point with:

  I<verb> Algorithm

  indicating you are expecting to plug in an algorithm.

- or, feature sequencers with:

  I<verb> Sequencer

  indicating that what you are expecting is indeed a sequencer.

Which approach is better? Or perhaps it is better to ask: which approach when?

The "kinds of classes" classification can be expressed with interfaces or with superclasses; after all, "is a kind of" is the central idea behind an effective subclass–superclass relationship. We usually take on the main problem-domain classification first, with inheritance. For other "kinds of classes" classifications, we use interface names built with a noun.

The "kinds of classes" interfaces work well for plug-in points at the end of an association or the end of a message—describing the full spectrum of interactions (more than just a "get" and a "set") along that path.

In contrast, the "kinds of behavior" interfaces work well for:

- little groupings of functionality within an "is a kind of" classification scheme, and

- the functionality required at an algorithmic plug-in point.

In practice, the most common "kinds of classes" names we use in object models correspond to the "pattern players" in the companion book, *Object Models: Strategies, Patterns, and Applications.* As class names, we can express those pattern players this way:

> Party, PartyRole
>
> Place, PlaceRole
>
> Thing, ThingRole
>
> Moment, Interval
>
> LineItem, ItemDescription, SpecificItem

Yet often we find that we want one of these categories (e.g., Role) to offer the same interface as another (e.g., Party) and so we end up using interfaces for such overlaps—and inheritance when we don't:

> IParty, PartyRole
>
> IPlace, PlaceRole
>
> IThing, ThingRole
>
> Moment, Interval
>
> LineItem, ItemDescription, ISpecificItem

Each of those "kinds of classes" classes and interfaces might consist of a number of little "kinds of behavior" interfaces, for example:

> IParty: IAddress, IConnectPartyRole, INameLegal, INumber, IPhone
>
> PartyRole: INumber, IConnectMoment
>
> where:
>
> IAddress: getAddress, setAddress
>
> IConnectMoment: addMoment, getMoment, removeMoment
>
> IConnectPartyRole: addRole, getRole, removeRole
>
> INameLegal: getNameLegal, setNameLegal
>
> INumber: getNumber, setNumber

Problem-domain objects need large-grain interfaces like IParty and IPlace—and occasionally a plug-in method interface like ITaxAlgorithm. In contrast, human-interaction objects often need fine-grained interfaces like IAddress and INumber.

Incidentally, using "kinds of classes" interfaces requires that some class provide the creation services for objects of that type, such a class is known as a factory (let it know what kind of object you need and it makes one up for you).

3.8   What Java Interfaces Lack

From a software designer's perspective, interfaces are the most important language construct in Java. As you've seen again and again in this chapter, interfaces open the door to remarkable design flexibility.

Yet, to make sure you leave this chapter with your feet firmly planted on *terra firma,* we wrap up this chapter with Java interface shortcomings.

Java interfaces specify method signatures and nothing more. And that's just not enough. James Gosling knows this; he included assertions in the last Java spec he wrote himself, took them out during a schedule crunch, and regrets having done so (as reported in an interview in *JavaWorld,* in March 1998).

We really should have syntax for three kinds of assertions, so we can express:

- The conditions for invoking a particular method (method preconditions)

- The conditions that an object satisfy at the end of a particular method (method postconditions)

- The conditions that an object must satisfy at the end of *any* method execution (commonly referred to as class invariants).

You see, there is a whole world of implied context for each and every plug-in point that you establish with an interface. Each plug-in point is like an integrated-circuit socket on a circuit board.

1. Someone decided the added flexibility was worth the added cost of establishing that plug-in point.

2. Someone expects that whatever is plugged into that socket will abide by certain rules and conventions.

For Java plug-in points, interfaces, it would be great if you could express that context explicitly, with programming language syntax for preconditions, postconditions, and assertions (the programming language Eiffel sets the standard here). We hope to see Java include such syntax at some point in the future.

3.9 Summary

In this chapter you've worked with interfaces: common sets of method signatures that you define for use again and again in your application.

Designing with interfaces is the most significant aspect of Java-inspired design because it gives you freedom from associations that are hardwired to just one class of objects and freedom from scenario interactions that are hardwired to objects in just one class. For systems in which flexibility, extensibility, and pluggability are key issues, Java-style interfaces are a must. Indeed the larger the system and the longer the potential life span of a system, the more significant interface-centric design becomes.

In this chapter, you've learned and applied the following specific strategies for designing better apps:

Challenge Each Association Strategy: *Is this association hardwired only to objects in that class (simpler), or is this an association to any object that implements a certain interface (more flexible, extensible, pluggable)?*

Challenge Each Message-Send Strategy: *Is this message-send hardwired only to objects in that class (simpler), or is this a message-send to any object that implements a certain interface (more flexible, extensible, pluggable)?*

Factor Out Repeaters Strategy: *Factor out method signatures that repeat within your class diagram. Resolve synonyms into a single signature. Generalize overly specific names into a single signature. Rea-*

sons for use: to explicitly capture the common, reusable behavior and to bring a higher level of abstraction into the model.

Factor Out to a Proxy Strategy: *Factor out method signatures into a proxy, an object with a solo association to some other object. Reason for use: to simplify the proxy within a class diagram and its scenarios (Figure 3-9).*

Factor Out for Analogous Apps Strategy: *Factor out method signatures that could be applicable in analogous apps. Reason for use: to increase likelihood of using and reusing off-the-shelf classes.*

Factor Out for Future Expansion Strategy: *Factor out method signatures now, so objects from different classes can be graciously accommodated in the future. Reason for use: to embrace change flexibility.*

Where to Add Interfaces Strategy: *Add interfaces at those points in your design that you anticipate change: (1) Connect with an interface implementer rather than with an object in a specific class; (2) Send a message to an interface implementer rather than to an object in a specific class; and (3) Invoke a plug-in method rather than a method defined within a class.*

Design-in, from Features to Interfaces Strategy:

1. *Look for a common feature, one you need to provide in different contexts.*

2. *Identify a set of method names that correspond to that feature.*

3. *Add an interface.*

4. *Identify implementers.*

Design-in, from Role Doubles to Interfaces Strategy:

1. *Take a role and turn its method signatures into a role-inspired interface.*

2. *Let another role (a "role double") offer that same interface by:*

- *implementing that interface, and*

- *delegating the real work back to the original role player.*

Design-in, from Collections and Members to Interfaces Strategy:

1. *Does your object hold a collection of other objects? If so:*

   a. *Consider the potential "across the collection" method signatures.*

   b. *If other collections might offer the same set of method signatures, then design in that common interface.*

2. *Is your object a member within a collection? If so:*

   If that object needs to provide an interface similar to the collections it is in, then design in that common interface.

3. *Identify implementers.*

Design-in, from Scenarios to Interfaces Strategy:

1. *Look for similar interactions.*

2. *Add an interface-implementer column.*

   Use this naming convention:

   I<what it does> Implementer.

3. *Add an interface: I<what it does>.*

4. *Identify implementers.*

Interface Granularity Strategy: *If a method signature can only exist with others, then add it directly to an interface definition with those others (no need for a separate, one-signature interface).*

Design-in, from Intra-class Roles to Interfaces Strategy:

1. *Identify roles that objects within a class can play.*

2. *Establish an interface for each of those roles.*

3. *Identify implementers.*

When to Use Plug-in Algorithms and Interfaces Strategy: *Use a plug-in algorithm and interface when you find this combination of problems:*

- *An algorithm you want to use can vary from object to object within a single class*

- *An algorithm is complex enough that you cannot drive its variation using attribute values alone.*

- *An algorithm is different for different categories of objects within a class—and even within those categories (hence, adding a category-description class won't resolve this problem).*

- *An algorithm you want to use will be different over time and you don't know at this point what all those differences will be.*

Design-in, from Plug-in Algorithms to Interfaces Strategy:

1. *Look for useful functionality you'd like to "plug in."*

2. *Add a plug-in point, using an interface.*

3. *Identify implementers.*

Chapter 4

Design with Threads

This chapter is about concurrency—doing more than one thing at a time.

4.1 Threads

4.1.1 What Is a Thread?

A thread is a single stream of program execution—one statement after the next after the next (see Figure 4-1).

Multiple threads are more than one stream of program execution running in parallel, or concurrently. The program runs one statement after the next after the next—and then switches to a different part of the program and runs one statement after the next after the next—and then switches to a different part of the program and runs one statement after the next after the next, and so on.

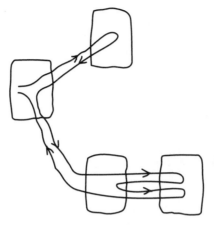

Figure 4-1. A single thread, winding its way through some objects.

Multiple threads might follow the same path (Figure 4-2) or different paths (Figure 4-3) as they wind their way through a program.

4.1.2 How Do Threads Get Started?

How do threads get started, and with how many threads am I working?

Here's one way to start a thread: begin with a UI object (Figure 4-4). Each client has its own thread, so with multiple clients you have multiple threads; your design must account for this.

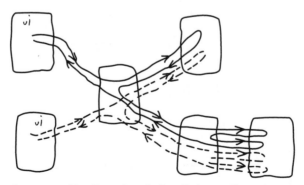

Figure 4-2. Two threads, winding their way through some objects.

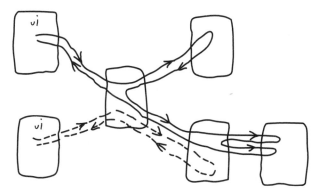

Figure 4-3. Two threads, winding their way on different paths through some objects.

Here's another way to start a thread: begin with a thread object (Figure 4-4). Thread objects, you say? Yes. In Java, there is a class called Thread. You can ask the class to create a new thread object for you. Then you can tell that thread object to start—and (along with other threads) that thread will begin (at whatever starting point you give it) and wind its way through objects in your app.

Cool, huh?

So you add thread objects when you need additional program streams above and beyond a single programming stream for each

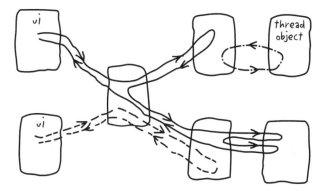

Figure 4-4. Two threads beginning from UI objects, one thread beginning from a thread object.

client. Why? If you need to give the appearance of doing more than one thing at a time, thread objects are the tools you need to use to get the job done. For example, at Zoe's Zones, we could run monitoring at a high level of priority (in one thread), yet let assessing of reliability run at a lower level of priority (in another).

It's helpful to think of a *thread object* like any other object when asking a thread to start, stop, and the like.

It's helpful to visualize a *thread* as something that starts from a client or a thread object and then winds its way through your application.

4.1.3   Why Use Multiple Threads?

Most designs must account for multiple streams of program execution; this chapter shows how to do that safely.

Multiple threads let you give the appearance of doing more than one thing at a time. For example, your application can serve multiple clients at the same time, or you can spawn a background printing thread (while still allowing the user to continue interacting with the foreground thread).

Threads also give you a clean, simple way to design in the main thing you want your application to do, along with other things that you'd like it to be aware of or check on from time to time (like a background calculation or some other mundane chore).

Threads simplify a design when you need to give the appearance that you are doing more than one thing at a time (Figure 4-5). Threads also improve response time when a higher priority part of an application needs to run.

4.1.4   If You Don't Need Multiple Threads, Don't Use Them

If you don't need to give the appearance of doing more than one thing at a time, don't use multiple threads.

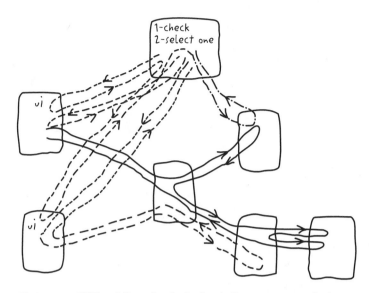

Figure 4-5.   Without threads, designing in the appearance that you are doing more than one thing at a time gets complicated in a hurry!

Why?

First and foremost, keep your design simple. By doing one thing at a time and not creating conflicts between shared resources, all will be well.

Secondly keep your overhead down. Multiple threads add processing overhead, the time it takes to change from one thread to the next; it's called context switch time. Your app eats up some microseconds each time it switches from one thread to another. It adds up.

4.1.5   Sync

In Java, a "sync'd" method is *synchronized* in the following way:

- only one thread is allowed in at a time

- only one thread is allowed in any sync'd method within a given object

- a thread within a sync'd method can invoke nonsync'd methods

- a thread within a sync'd method can invoke sync'd methods within the same object, immediately entering into that method without delay

- a thread within a sync'd method can invoke sync'd methods in another object, but if another thread is already inside, it must wait in a queue just like any other thread.

4.1.6   Sync: A Guarantee and a Nonguarantee

A sync guarantees that only one thread will run within *a method* for *an object*, making it "thread-safe."

However, a sync has a nonguarantee when it comes to good service: any other threads that come along to invoke sync'd methods within that object wait in a queue, standing by until the earlier threads exit the sync'd method (Figure 4-6).

Other threads, running in other objects, even running in the same object (winding their way through nonsync'd methods), continue to run. Those other threads get turns running, perhaps even before the thread that was running in a sync'd method gets the opportunity to complete ending that sync (the thread with the highest priority in the waiting queue always goes first).

Hence, a sync *does not* guarantee that a thread will run to completion before being interrupted by another thread somewhere else in the application.

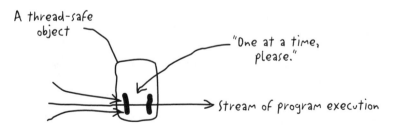

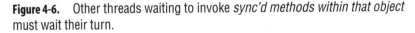

Figure 4-6.   Other threads waiting to invoke *sync'd methods within that object* must wait their turn.

4.1.7 Sync: Scope

You can sync an instance method so that just one thread at a time can enter and work with the values of its instance variables.

You can sync a class method so that just one thread at a time can enter and work with the values of its class variables.*

4.1.8 Shared Value (and Keeping Out of Trouble)

Threads and tasks (real-time processes) are very similar. Okay then, in what few ways are they different? Threads share the same set of values in a running program; each task has its own set of values (Figure 4-7).

Consequently, the overhead for threads is lower. All newer operating systems support threads; it's the trendy way to support concurrency.

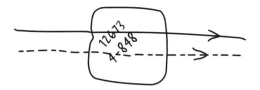

Figure 4-7. Threads share the same internal values.

---

*In Java, you can even sync a block of code within a method. A better idea is to put that code in a separate method because you'll end up with smaller, more cohesive methods (a good idea) and harder-to-miss sync's (also a good idea).

An object with one or more sync'd methods has a lock. When a thread enters one of its sync'd methods, the lock for that object is set (no other thread can enter that sync'd method or any other sync'd method for that object). When a thread exits a sync'd method, the lock for that object is reset. (Similarly, this is true for a class with one or more sync'd class methods.)

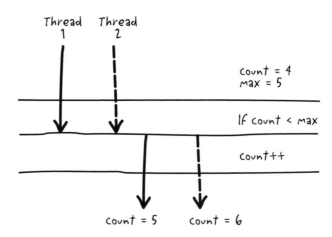

Figure 4-8.   Why methods that work with internal values must be sync'd.

Consequently, as designers we have to make sure that multiple threads don't work with the same values at the same time. Otherwise, we might get unexpected results (Figure 4-8).

In Figure 4-8:

- Internal values of the object are set to count = 4, max = 5
- Thread 1 executes the first part of the statement:

    if 4 < 5   (count < max)

- Thread 2 gets a turn and executes the first part of the same statement:

    if 4 < 5   (count < max)

- Thread 1 executes the second part of the statement:

    5 = 4 + 1   (count ++)

- Thread 2 gets a turn and executes the same statement:

    6 = 5 + 1   (count ++)

Yes, a thread might get through just part of a statement. Why? Because each Java statement becomes some number of bytecodes. The Java virtual machine executes one bytecode at a time. Most often, threads *are* interrupted in the middle of a Java statement.

And so, in this case, the count ends up with a value greater than max, which is not at all what we expected.

How do we get around this problem?

Methods that work with internal values must be sync'd (sometimes referred to as "locked"), meaning that such methods should allow just one thread in at a time.

Syncs add processing overhead, so it's not a good idea to sync everything in sight.

However, keep in mind that if you don't sync up something that you should, values can become corrupted, leading to erroneous results.

Checking your design for being "thread-safe" is an important aspect of designing with multiple threads.

Sync Access to Values Strategy: When multiple threads compete for value(s) within an object—and you try other thread paths but cannot avoid competition for these values—use sync'd methods to limit access (one thread at a time). For multithreaded objects, sync each method that compares, operates on, gets, or sets internal values.

4.1.9   Don't Sync Longer Than You Have To

The idea in a multithreaded design is to let multiple threads run through your application.

When you sync a method and a thread enters that sync, then *no other thread can enter any sync'd method in that object* until that sync method runs to completion. It's similar to a multilane highway that suddenly squeezes down to just one lane: if traffic is light, no problem; if traffic is heavy, the queue stretches out for miles and miles.

This means that it's a good idea to streamline a sync'd method, including just those steps that must be sync'd.

Zoom In and Sync Strategy: Zoom in on exactly what you need to sync, factor it out into a separate method, and sync that method. Why? Sync for as little time as possible so other (potentially higher priority) threads waiting at the start of other sync methods for that object will get to run sooner rather than later.

4.1.10 Shared Resource (and Keeping Out of Trouble)

Too many syncs can hang your application.

Watch out for a sync'd method that extends its reach to other methods. If that thread hits another sync'd method in some other object and another thread is inside, then it must wait—and might be stuck forever.* Welcome to the wonderful world of deadlock (Figure 4-9).

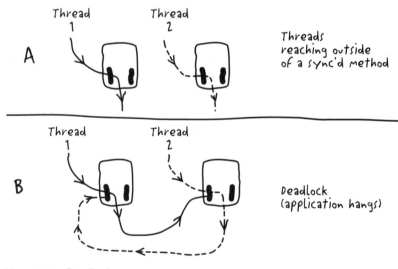

Figure 4-9.   Deadlock.

---

*A thread can re-acquire a lock on an object that it already locked, even if others are waiting. This avoids any possibility of a circular deadlock and allows synchronized methods within the same object to call one another.

Here's how deadlock happens:

Thread 1 enters a sync'd method. Then, before exiting that sync'd method, it follows a method call outside of that object.

Thread 2 enters a sync'd method. Then, before exiting that sync'd method, it follows a method call outside of that object.

Thread 1 arrives at the sync'd method that Thread 2 already entered, and waits for Thread 2 to exit that method.

Thread 2 arrives at the sync'd method that Thread 1 already entered, and waits for Thread 1 to exit that method.

You can find deadlock in everyday life (for example, TCP/IP), although usually someone gives in and allows it to end (Figure 4-10).

A pair of strategies is needed here, analogous to "when to sync access to values" and "how to sync access to values."

This time, it's at a bit higher level of abstraction.

Sync Access to Objects Strategy: *When multiple threads compete for entry into each other's sync'd methods, use a gatekeeper to control access one thread at a time, and make sure the objects that the gatekeeper protects have no sync methods.*

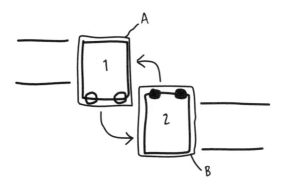

Figure 4-10. Deadlock at the mall, each car sync'd one space, then waited at each other's sync'd space (with some drivers, this deadlock could last forever).

What can you do about deadlock like the one shown in Figure 4-10? Add an object that acts as a gatekeeper; design the object interactions so that each thread first sync's on a gatekeeper's method, followed by exclusive sync'd access to the objects that the gatekeeper protects.

In a parking lot, you can add a gatekeeper by (1) adding a very stern parking attendant or (2) slanting the parking slots to encourage one-way travel down the rows in the parking lot (one-way streets in large cities have a similar effect).

4.2   Multiple Clients, Multiple Threads within an Object

Back to Charlie's Charters and its reservation system.

As soon as the reservation system has more than one agent making reservations at the same time, then we have multiple clients and multiple threads.

Here it's not a matter of whether or not to use multiple threads; multiple threads are definitely part of the design.

Here, it's a matter of using multiple threads safely. Hmmm. It sounds like it is time for a couple of strategies:

Value Gatekeeper Strategy: *Look for a method that increments or decrements a count of a limited resource. Sync that method; give it exclusive access to that count.*

Object Gatekeeper Strategy: *Look for a method that reserves or issues a limited resource, represented by the objects in that collection. Sync that method and give it exclusive access to that collection of objects.*

Apply these strategies to Charlie's Charters.

What limited resource are we working with? Space on a scheduled flight.

Do we manage a counter or a collection of objects? If we had a seat map and made seat assignments, then we'd have a collection of objects. But at Charlie's Charters, all we have is a counter, the count of the number of reservations on the flight.

So, based upon the "value gatekeeper" strategy, we'd expect to sync a method within the ScheduledFlight class.

Figure 4-11 illustrates what the object model looks like.

Sync the method responsible for comparing the current number of reservations against the capacity and adding in the new reservation. It's the "try to add reservation" method.

Figure 4-12 depicts the scenario.

In Java, it looks like this:

```
public class ScheduledFlight {

    // attributes / private / associations
    private Vector reservations = new Vector();
```

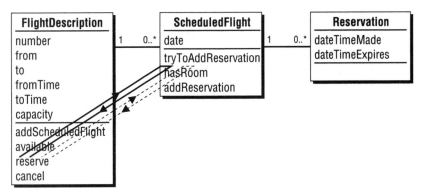

Figure 4-11   Multiple threads could lead to inadvertent overbooking. You need to sync here.

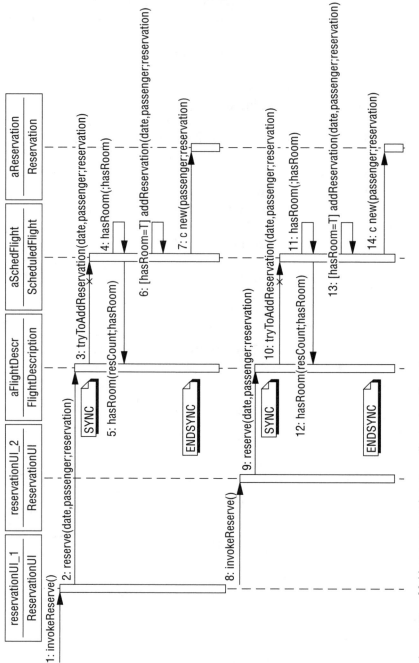

Figure 4-12. Making a reservation: two clients, two threads.

```
// methods / public / conducting business
public synchronized
        Reservation tryToAddReservation(
                Date aDate, Passenger aPassenger) {
        // code goes here
        if (this.hasRoom()){
                // code goes here
                this.addReservation(aDate, aPassenger);}
        /* code goes here */ }

// methods / protected / conducting business
protected boolean hasRoom() {
        /* code goes here */ }
protected Reservation addReservation (
        Date aDate, Passenger aPassenger) {
        /* code goes here */ }
}
```

Code notes: This code limits the visibility of hasRoom and addReservation and only calls them within a synchronized method. If one could add a reservation without first having to check if there's room, then one could synchronize addReservation. The reservations vector is the resource that this code protects.

4.3   Multiple Thread Objects, Multiple Threads within an Object

Now let's take a look at Zoe's Zones.

We're working with zones and sensors. This time, we're beginning with just one thread and considering when and if we might add additional threads. Here is a helpful strategy:

Four Thread Designs Strategy: Apply these thread designs, looking for the simplest one that will satisfy your performance requirements. From simplest to most complex, consider: (1) single thread, (2) prioritized-object threads, (3) prioritized-method threads, (4) prioritized-method prioritized-object threads.

4.3.1   Single Thread

The simplest solution is a single-thread design.

It's not high-tech sexy. After all, threads and concurrency are really fun things to mess around with. But wait a minute. We're not in a classroom. We're not considering a group of dining philosophers who like sharing their eating utensils with each other. We're designing an application.

A simpler design is a better design provided that it gets the job done within time, budget, and resource constraints.

Could a single-thread solution work here? Let's take a closer look (Figure 4-13).

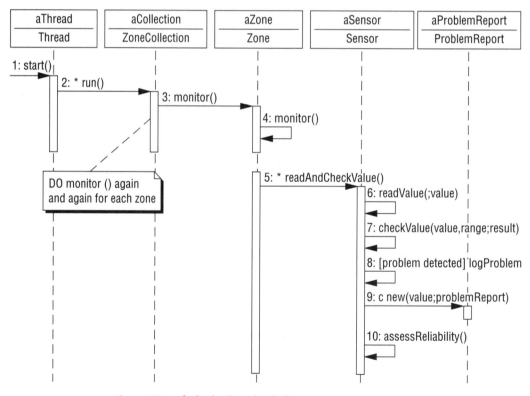

Figure 4-13.   A single-thread solution.

Someone creates a thread object and asks it to start. At that point, the thread becomes runnable. When that runnable thread gets a turn to run, the thread object tells its corresponding zone object to run, and so the thread begins winding its way through the scenario.

In Java, it looks like this:

```
public class Zone implements Runnable {

    // attributes / private / thread
    private Thread mainThread;

    // attributes / private / associations
    private Vector sensors = new Vector();

    // methods / public / activation
    public void activate() {
        // create the main thread and start it
        this.mainThread = new Thread(this);
        this.mainThread.start(); }

    // methods / public / Runnable implementation
    public void run() {
        for(;;) { // loop forever until thread is stopped
            this.monitor(); } }

    // methods / public / conducting business
    public void monitor() {
        // iterate through the vector of sensors and tell each sensor to
        // readAndCheck
        Enumeration sensorList = this.sensors.elements();
        while (sensorList.hasMoreElements()) {
            // must cast the element to a Sensor
            Sensor aSensor = (Sensor)sensorList.nextElement();
            aSensor.readAndCheckValue(); } }

}
```

Code notes: This is just the snippet for Zone. To kick things off, this code has an activate method, which creates the main thread and asks the thread to start. The run method has an internal loop that will continue to call monitor until the main thread is stopped. The monitor method iterates through the vector of sensors, asking each one to read and check its value.

A single thread winds its way through each zone and its sensors. For each sensor, the thread reads a sensor, compares the reading with a threshold, logs any detected problems, and assesses sensor reliability.

Just one thread runs through the objects. There is no one to fight with, and nothing to fight over, so no sync's are needed.

This simplest design will work, if the thread can run around fast enough and get everything done on time.

But what if you have hundreds of zones and thousands of sensors? A single thread might still be okay.

You must look at how long it takes to run a single thread through every zone and its sensors and then compare it with the required sampling rate. If the processing time is 10 minutes (a very long time) and the sampling rate is once per hour, then a single-thread design will get the job done.

It's not elegant. It's not high-tech cool, but it is a cost-effective, more easily implemented solution. Come to think of it, that *is* high-tech cool.

4.3.2   Responsible Thread

Programming with threads is becoming a bit more refined in Java 1.2, in the sense that a thread object is the one that decides when to suspend or stop itself. In fact, the suspend, resume, and stop methods are deprecated, meaning that using those methods (and method names) in new software is discouraged.

In 1.2, rather than sending a suspend or stop message to a thread object and expect it to immediately carry out that request, you send something like a "requestSuspend" or requestStop" message and let the thread itself decide what to do. That thread object then checks to make sure that it is not holding any locks; when all is in order, that thread can suspend or stop itself.

This more object-centric approach makes it possible for a programmer to avoid lingering locks and potential deadlocks from those lingering locks.

In Java, it looks like this:

Code note: A "responsible thread" knows its own state and decides when it is safe to end itself. JDK 1.1 reinforces this object-centric perspective, deprecating the previously available suspend, resume, and stop methods.

```java
public class ResponsibleThread extends Thread {

    static final int RUN = 0;
    static final int SUSPEND = 1;
    static final int STOP = 2;
    private int state = RUN;
    public synchronized void setState(int s) {
        this.state = s;
        if (this.state == RUN)
            this.notify();
    }

    private synchronized boolean checkState() {
        while (this.state == SUSPEND) {
            try {
                wait();
            } catch (Exception e) {}
        }
        if (this.state == STOP) {
            return false;
        }
        return true;
    }
    public void run() {
        while (true) {
            // do something
            if (!checkState())    // thread ends itself
                break;
        }
    }
}
```

4.3.3 Prioritized-Object Threads

What if a single-thread solution is just not fast enough? Then what?

Mindlessly adding threads with the hope of making things run faster is an exercise in futility. Threads add overhead—context switch time, sync and end-sync times—and might actually slow down your app.

Multiple threads will save you time, and make the application appear to run faster, *if and only if* some threads can run at a higher priority than other threads.

One approach is to add threads within higher prioritized objects.

What are the priority objects in this system?

> Zone—low
>
> Some sensors—high
>
> Some sensors—medium

So use three prioritized-object threads.

This is a multithreaded solution, with multiple threads running through the same object. Sensor status is the attribute that both threads use.

In a multithreaded design, look for where threads intersect. Here, the threads intersect at the status of a sensor.

Let's use the "zoom in and sync" strategy to move in as close as we can. Rather than sync these large methods—sync readAndCheckValue and sync monitor—let's sync as close as possible to the intersection of these threads, a pair of methods that act as "value gatekeepers," namely, sync getStatus and sync setStatus (Figure 4-14). Note the additional X near the message arrow, indicating a message to a synchronized method.

In Java, it looks like this:

```
public class Zone implements Runnable {
```

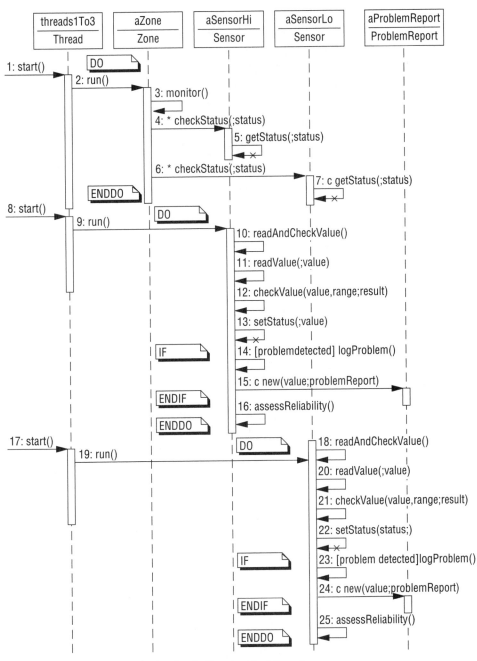

Figure 4-14. A trio of prioritized-*object* threads.

```
// attributes / private / thread
private ResponsibleThread myThread;

// attributes / private / object connections
private Vector sensors = new Vector();

// methods / public / activation
public void activate(int priority) {
    // create my thread and start it
    this.myThread = new ResponsibleThread(this);
    this.myThread.setPriority(priority);
    this.myThread.start(); }

// methods / public / Runnable implementation
public void run() {
    for(;;) { // loop forever until thread is stopped
        this.monitor();
        try {Thread.sleep(100); } catch(Interrupted Exception e) { } } }

// methods / public / conducting business
public void monitor() {
    // iterate through the vector of sensors and tell
    // each sensor to check Status
    Enumeration sensorList = this.sensors.elements();
    while (sensorList.hasMoreElements()) {
        // must cast the element to a Sensor
        Sensor aSensor = (Sensor)sensorList.nextElement();
        String status = aSensor.checkStatus();
        /* evaluate status */ } }

}
```

Code notes: This time, the activate method takes a parameter to set the priority of the thread. Also, because each sensor performs readAndCheckValue on its own thread, the code simply asks each sensor for its status.

```
public class Sensor implements Runnable {

    // attributes / private / thread
    private ResponsibleThread myThread;
```

```
// methods / public / activation
public void activate(int priority) {
    // create my thread and start it
    this.myThread = new ResponsibleThread(this);
    this.myThread.setPriority(priority);
    this.myThread.start(); }

// methods / public / Runnable implementation
public void run() {
    for(;;) { // loop forever until thread is stopped
        this.readAndCheckValue();
        try {thread.sleep(100);} catch(Interrupted Exception e){ } }}

// methods / public / conducting business
public String checkStatus() {
    /* code goes here */ }
// methods / protected synchronized / conducting business
protected synchronized String getStatus() { /* code goes here */ }
protected synchronized void setStatus(String status) {
    /* code goes here */ }

// methods / protected / conducting business
protected void readAndCheckValue() {
    /* code goes here
        calls the following methods:
            readValue, checkValue, logProblem, and assessReliability */ }
protected int readValue() { /* code goes here */ }
protected int checkValue(int value, Range aRange) { /* code goes here */ }
protected void logProblem() { /* code goes here */ }
protected boolean assessReliability() { /* code goes here */ }
```

✂

```
}
```

Code notes: This time, Sensor needs its own activate method and priority parameter, just like Zone. The code limits the visibility of most of the major conducting business methods. The only main public method, other than activate and
run, is the checkStatus method, which is invoked by a zone. The getStatus and
setStatus methods must be synchronized.

That looks just fine. However, there is an added problem that you
need to consider whenever you have different priorities for threads
with the same basic responsibilities; it's called "starvation."

Starvation occurs when a low-priority thread never gets a turn; this happens when high priority threads always keep the processor busy.

Starvation is not a problem if the amount of processing time is small compared to the total time available.

As processing time approaches total time available, the likelihood of starvation of one or more threads increases. If timely servicing of low-priority threads is not a big deal, then all is well.

In Zoe's case, starvation will cause zones to be starved of their monitoring behavior first, followed by the starvation of both monitoring and accessing behavior of the lower priority sensors. Not a good thing for Zoe or her customers.

If timely servicing of low-priority threads is important, however, then we've got two options to consider:

1. Add a thread manager. A thread manager can tell all high-priority threads to go to sleep for a short period of time, making sure that low-priority threads get executed along the way. It's like adding a socialized government to make sure everyone gets their share.

2. Don't use prioritized-object threads; we're merely applying a single-thread solution on a sensor-by-sensor basis; indeed, a single-thread solution would be simpler and faster.

4.3.4   Prioritized-Method Threads

We've tried single threads and prioritized-object threads.

However, if high-priority methods within some objects are still not getting executed in a timely fashion, we can take a look at another prioritization scheme: *give execution priority to those methods.*

Here's how to do it:

Prioritized-Methods Strategy: *Prioritize your methods. Separate out cohesive functions with different priorities. Run higher priority methods in higher priority threads; run lower priority methods in lower priority threads.*

The higher priority thread, now relieved of doing lower priority work, will run in less time. So in places where a single-thread approach fails because it's not fast enough, prioritized-method threads can save the day.

The cost? Some added design complexity is required, but it is well worth it.

What are the method priorities in this system?

Monitor zone—low

Assess sensor reliability—medium

Monitor sensor—high

What if the sampling rate for reading sensors is so fast that at times we just cannot keep up?

The key words here are "at times." After all, if you are always too slow, time-averaging some of the work will be of no help at all.

If you cannot keep up at times, you can spin off lower priority work into a separate thread (or threads), and then let the app catch up on that work after a while.

For sensor monitoring, you could strip it down to "read and save a sample" and then let another thread take care of "checking and logging a problem report, if any."

We'll pursue that design in Chapter 5.

For now, stick with three prioritized-method threads: monitor zone, assess sensor reliability, and monitor sensor (Figure 4-15).

This is another multithreaded solution, with multiple threads running through the same object (sensor). Sensor status is the attribute that all threads use.

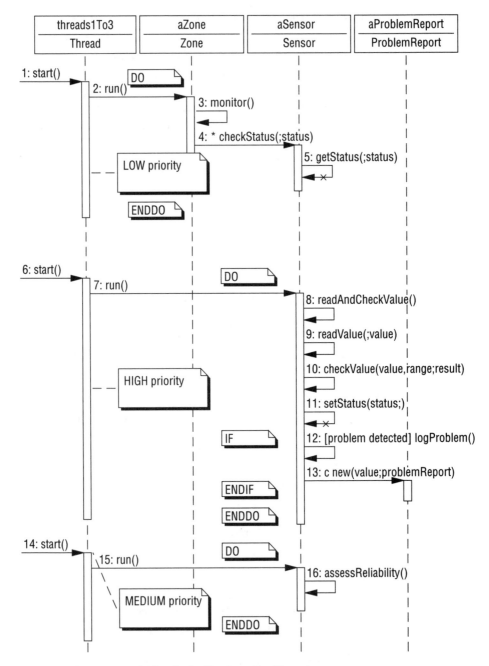

Figure 4-15. A trio of prioritized-*method* threads.

In Java, it looks like this:

```java
public class Sensor implements Runnable {

    // attributes / private / threads
    private ResponsibleThread monitoringThread;
    private ResponsibleThread assessingThread;

    // methods / public / activation
    public void activate(int monitoringPriority, int assessingPriority) {
        // create monitoring thread and start it
        this.monitoringThread = new ResponsibleThread(this);
        this.monitoringThread.setPriority(monitoringPriority);
        this.monitoringThread.start();
        // create assessing thread and start it
        this.assessingThread = new ResponsibleThread(this);
        this.assessingThread.setPriority(assessingPriority);
        this.assessingThread.start(); }

    // methods / public / Runnable implementation
    public void run() {
        // if the current thread entering run is the monitoring thread,
        // then read and check until stopped.
        if (Thread.currentThread()== this.monitoringThread ) {
            for(;;) { // loop forever until thread is stopped
                this.readAndCheck();
                try {Thread.sleep(100);} catch(InterruptedException e){ } } }

        // else if the current thread entering run is the assessing thread,
        // then assess reliability until stopped
        if (Thread.currentThread()== this.assessingThread ) {
            for(;;) { // loop forever until thread is stopped
                this.assessReliability();
                try {Thread.sleep(100);} catch(InterruptedException e){ } } }

    // methods / public / conducting business
    public String checkStatus() {
        /* code goes here */ }

    // methods / protected synchronized / conducting business
    protected synchronized String getStatus() { /* code goes here */ }
```

```
protected synchronized void setStatus(String status) {
    /* code goes here */ }

// methods / protected / conducting business
protected void readAndCheckValue() {
    /* code goes here
      calls the following methods:
         readValue, checkValue, and logProblem. */ }
protected int readValue() { /* code goes here */ }
protected int checkValue(int value, Range aRange) { /* code goes here */ }
protected void logProblem() { /* code goes here */ }
protected boolean assessReliability() { /* code goes here */ }

}
```

Code notes: The Zone remains the same. Sensor's activate method now takes two parameters: one for the monitoring thread priority and one for the assessing thread priority. The run method checks the current thread and performs the appropriate loop. This time, the readAndCheckValue method does not call the assessReliability method because this method has its own thread.

4.3.5   Prioritized-Method Prioritized-Object Threads

You've tried single threads, prioritized-method threads, and prioritized-object threads.

However, if the simpler approaches won't get the job done, if you need maximum prioritization flexibility, then you can prioritize methods *and* objects.

If you have some methods that are more important than others, and if you have some objects that are more important than others, and if processing time is approaching actual time, then consider this approach carefully.

Based on prioritized methods, what threads do you need, and what are the relative priorities?

Monitor sensor, across all sensors—high

Assess sensor reliability, across all sensors—medium

Monitor zone, across all zones—low

Based on prioritized objects, what threads do you need, and what are the relative priorities?

> High-priority sensors—high
>
> Low-priority sensors—medium
>
> Zone—low

Merging these lists yields five kinds of threads in this design:

> Monitor a high-priority sensor—very high
>
> Monitor a low-priority sensor—high
>
> Assess a high-priority sensor—medium
>
> Assess a low-priority sensor—low
>
> Monitor a zone—very low.

Notice that monitoring *lower* priority sensors is still at a higher level of priority than assessing the reliability of the *higher* priority sensors. In this way, all monitoring runs at a higher level of priority than any assessing.

Hence, the overall thread count for this design works out to

> One thread per zone object
>
> Two threads per high-priority or low-priority sensor

That's a lot, it's true. This is an extreme case. The good thing about this design is that it's got room for a lot of fine tuning and tweaking. The bad thing about this design is that it uses lots and lots of threads, which isn't a good thing, unless it must be done to meet system response time requirements for high-priority sensors. Hence, the following strategy:

Thread Count Strategy: *Justify the existence of each thread in your design. If you can reduce the thread count and meet response time requirements, do so.*

Figure 4-16 depicts a scenario that represents six threads, two zones, two priorities of sensors, two thread priorities within each sensor, and a partridge in a pear tree.

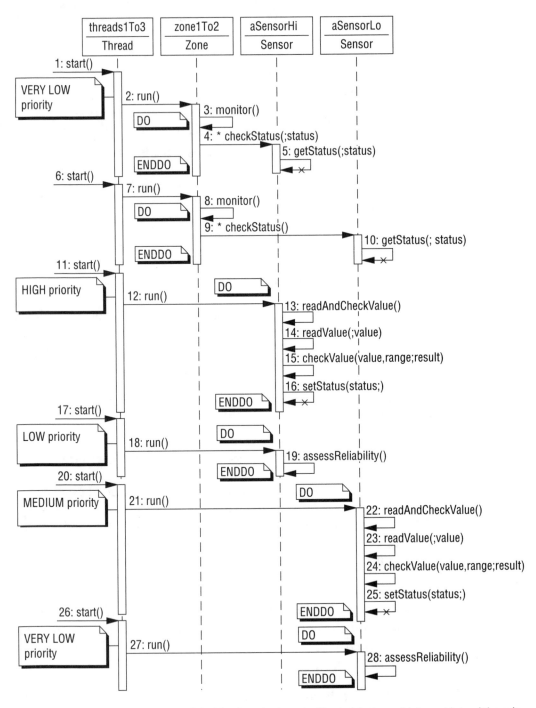

Figure 4-16. Prioritized methods, prioritized objects, and lots and lots of threads.

In Java, it looks like this:

Code notes: It's the same source code as in the previous example. When creating sensors, adjust the priority parameters in the activate method so that high-priority sensors have a higher monitoring priority than low-priority sensors. Make sure that the assessing priority for the high-priority sensors is lower than the monitoring priority for the low-priority sensors, or low-priority sensors may not have enough processing time to perform their monitoring. For example:

```
// set monitoring priority to 8 and assessing priority to 3
Sensor aSensorHi = new Sensor();
aSensorHi.activate(8,3);
// set monitoring priority to 7 and assessing priority to 2
Sensor aSensorLo = new Sensor();
aSensorLo.activate(7,2);
```

This approach allows the greatest flexibility and lots of room for fine tuning.

4.3.6   Overall Point

The overall point here is keep it simple.

Use a single-thread design whenever you can.

If you cannot get the job done that way, then you've got to prioritize what you do. Identify priority methods, adding submethods to separate out cohesive functions with different priorities. Give priority to certain objects. Give priority to certain methods. Or give priority to both.

4.4   Interface Adapters

Designing with threads is an advanced design topic. Designing with interface adapters is even more advanced. So, depending on your background in this area, you might opt to jump ahead to the summary at the end of this chapter and tackle this section another day.

Let's explore the wonderful world of interface adapters.

4.4.1   Need

A thread object is rather single minded in what it communicates to another object. A thread object sends a "run" message. That's it.

So what happens if multiple thread objects want to message the same object but yet invoke different methods for each one?

4.4.2   One Approach: Dispatcher

One approach is to add a test and a case statement to the run method (Figure 4-17).

The test statement asks a thread class which thread has just entered. The case statement routes the thread to the method it really needs to be running through.

However, a "case" statement at the beginning of any method implies some pretty lame internal cohesion.

A thread should be able to invoke the method it needs. If multiple threads want to invoke different methods in the same object, however, we need to add an intermediary: an interface adapter.

4.4.3   A Better Approach: Interface Adapters

Why not let each thread invoke the method it really wants to invoke rather than just a "run" method?

But how can you do this, when a thread implements the Runnable interface (run) rather than an application-specific message?

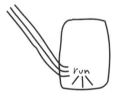

Figure 4-17.   Threads wanting to invoke different methods, but they're being forced through one entry point.

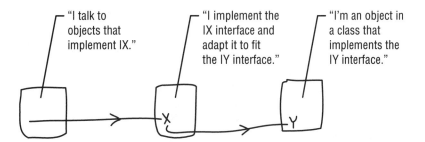

Figure 4-18. An interface adapter adapts interfaces.

The answer is use an interface adapter (Figure 4-18).

A sender tells an adapter to do something; that adapter translates the method call in one interface to another interface. Hence, the adapter is called an "interface adapter."

4.4.4   What an Interface Adapter Looks Like

Figure 4-19 illustrates an object-model pattern, the interface-adapter pattern.

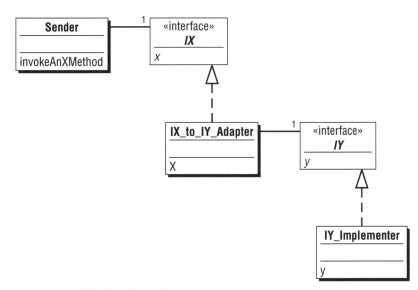

Figure 4-19. The interface-adapter pattern.

Note that the interface names in Figure 4-19 are not really interface names at all. They are abstractions of interface names that you might use when applying this pattern in a specific context.

The specific interfaces you choose to use will be different for each kind of interface-adapter class that you define for your application. For Zoe's Zones, we'll use this pattern to model something called, "thread–Runnable-to-IMonitor adapter–sensors." Before we do that, however, let's take a look at the scenario view for this pattern so we can consider its stereotypical interactions.

A receiver

- sends a message to create an interface adapter and it

- sends a message to create a sender (sending an interface adapter as an argument).

Then a sender sends a message to its "IX-to-IY" adapter. And finally, that interface adapter sends a message to its object that implements the "IY" interface.

This is illustrated in Figure 4-20.

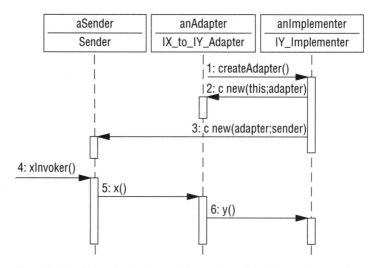

Figure 4-20.   Stereotypical interactions for an interface-adapter pattern.

In Java, it looks like this:

```
public interface IX {
    void x(); }
public interface IY {
    void y(); }

public class Sender {
✂
    // attributes / private / association
    private IX myIX;

    // methods / public / conducting business
    public void xInvoker() {
        // send the message x to myIX
        this.myIX.x(); }

    // constructors
    public Sender(IX anIX) {
        // set myIX to anIX
        this.myIX = anIX; }
✂
}

public class IX_to_IY_Adapter implements IX {
✂
    // attributes / private / association
    private IY myIY;

    // methods / public / IX implementation
    public void x () {
        // send the message y to myIY
        this.myIY.y(); }

    // constructors
    public IX_to_IY_Adapter (IY anIY) {
        // set myIY to anIY
        this.myIY = anIY; }
✂
}
```

```
public class IY_Implementer implements IY {
%
    // attributes / private / object connections
    private IX_to_IY_Adapter myAdapter;
    private Sender mySender;

    // methods / public / adapter creation
    public void createAdapter () {
        // create an adapter and pass myself as the parameter
        this.myAdapter = new IX_to_IY_Adapter(this);
        // create a sender and pass myAdapter as the parameter
        this.mySender = new Sender(this.myAdapter); }

    // methods / public / IY implementation
    public void y() { /* code goes here */ }
%
}
```

When should you use interface adapters for threads? Only when you need them. When do you need them? In the context of working with thread objects, you need interface adapters whenever you have multiple thread objects that you would like to invoke different methods in an object. And in a broader context, they are needed whenever you want to adapt a message-send from one object into some other message-send that is suitable for another object.

This is a good design, but consider what happens to your model shape if you need dozens (or hundreds) of adapter classes. Those adapters chew up a lot of model real estate while adding very little added value.

JDK 1.1 introduced inner classes so that one can design in adapter classes without the need for separate .java files. There are four kinds of inner classes. For adapters, *member classes* (and their variants) are the ones to focus-in on. The four kinds of inner classes are:

1. Nested top-level class (or interface)

    - Is a convenient way of grouping related classes/interfaces.

    - Is a packaging (encapsulation) mechanism.

- Is defined as static within an enclosing top-level class or interface

- Behaves like a normal class or interface

- Is referenced by including enclosing class name (Outer-Class.InnerClass)

2a. Member class

- Is a convenient way of grouping related classes/interfaces

- Is a more closely coupled packaging (encapsulation) mechanism

- Is not defined as static

- Can directly use attributes and methods in the enclosing class

- Automatically gets a reference to the enclosing object

2b. Local class

- Is just like a member class, except it's local (like a local variable is local)

- Is defined within a block of Java code

- Is only visible within that block of code

2c. Anonymous class

- Is just like a local class, except it's not given a name and is usually very short (that is to say, the declaration and instantiation are often just one line of code)

- Can be instantiated only once per execution of the block it's in

- Is used right after it's defined

- Cannot have its own constructor

- Is really nameless (meaning, an explicit class name does not add to understandability of the design, for example, simple adapters, simple listeners)

Some observations on the four kinds of inner classes:

- A nested class is a physical packaging and nothing more; it lets you use a class name as a package name. Include both the outer and nested classes in your model with the nested class name scoped this way: OuterClass.InnerClass.

- Member classes, local classes, and anonymous classes are nearly the same thing. The only real difference is the lack of class name and where you put it in your code (and hence, what variables it can directly access). One notation will suffice for all three.

A *member class* is perfect for adapter. With it, you can place an adapter inside of the class for which it is doing the adapting.

In this example, it means that you can place:

　　IX_to_IY_Adapter

inside of the class:

　　IY_Implementation.

Also, the adapter is a bit simpler this way, since it does not need to implement an association to the class for which it is doing the adapting. That association is provided automatically, by its being a member class, nested inside the other class and having an implicit reference to the enclosing object.

With a member class, the model looks like Figure 4-21.

In Java, here's what it looks like, implementing the adapter with a member class:

```
public interface IX {
    void x(); }

public interface IY {
    void y(); }
```

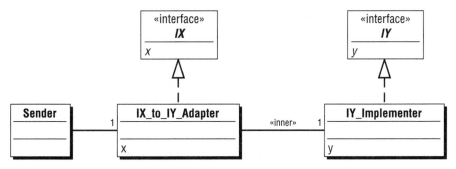

Figure 4-21. The interface-adapter pattern, using a member class for the adapter (UML notation does not specify a notation for member classes; here is one way to show them).

```
public class Sender {
    // attributes / private / association
    private IX myIX;

    // methods / public / conducting business
    public void xInvoker() {
        // send the message x to myIX
        this.myIX.x(); }

    // constructors
    public Sender(IX anIX) {
        // set myIX to anIX
        this.myIX = anIX; }
}

public class IY_Implementer / association implements IY {
    // attributes / private
    private Sender mySender;

    // constructors
        public IY_Implementer () {
        // create an adapter
        IX_to_IY_Adapter myAdapter = new IX_to_IY_Adapter();
        // create a sender and pass myAdapter as the parameter
        this.mySender = new Sender(myAdapter); }
```

```
        // methods / public / IY implementation
        public void y() { /* code goes here */ }

        // Implement the adapter as a member class
        class IX_to_IY_Adapter implements IX {
            // No member variable or constructor is required
            // The inner class automatically maintains a reference
            // to the enclosing class.
            // methods / public / IX implementation
            public void x () {
                // send the message y to my enclosing object
                y(); }
        }
}
```

This is how to implement the adapter as an anonymous class:

```
public class IY_Implementer implements IY {

// constructors

public IY_Implementer (Sender mySender)
    {
        // create an adapter, an instance of an anonymous
        // class (which implements the IX interface)
        IX myAdapter = new IX ()
        {  // here's the body of the anonymous inner class
        public void x () {
            // send the message y (instead of the message x)
            // to my enclosing object
            y(); }
        };  // note this semi-colon terminates the assignment statement
    }

// Pass the instance of the anonymous class to the Sender,
// using its addReceiver method.
 mySender.addReceiver(myAdapter); }

        // methods / public / IY implementation
        public void y() { /* code goes here */ }
}
```

Can we use inner classes everywhere? No. The added packaging must pay for itself in terms of understandability. Use inner classes when you have lots of adapters and want to encapsulate each adapter with what it adapts. Don't use inner classes when you have just a handful of adapters in an application.

4.4.5 Interface Adapters for Zoe's Zones

Here is what happens for Zoe's Zones for the "prioritized methods" approach.

You need threads to wind through each of the following:

A zone-monitoring thread

A sensor-monitoring thread

A sensor-assessing thread

4.4.6 A Zone-Monitoring Thread

A zone-monitoring thread needs no interface adapter because there is only one method to service—the "monitor" method. See Figure 4-22 for the scenario.

Note that the Zone class implements the Runnable interface, so a thread object can send a zone object a "run" message.

4.4.7 A Sensor-Assessing Thread and a Sensor-Monitoring Thread

Get ready for the next scenario.

Now you can apply the interface-adapter pattern. Applied in this context, the pattern looks like Figure 4-23.

Hmmm. You need a class that will implement the IMonitor interface. An object in that class will know all of the sensor objects in the application.

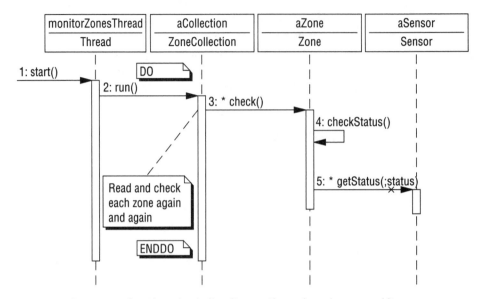

Figure 4-22. One thread, winding its way through each zone and its sensors.

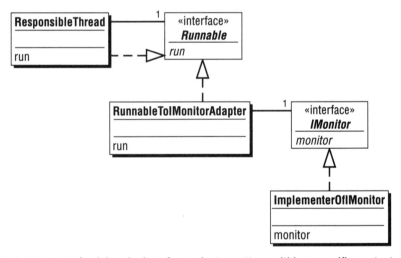

Figure 4-23. Applying the interface-adapter pattern within a specific context.

Note that normally you could embed this "across the collection" responsibility within the Sensor class itself (making sure that, upon creating a sensor object, you add it to that collection).

But here you are dealing with interfaces. And (Java-style) interfaces are intended for instance signatures rather than class method signatures. The impact in a scenario is minimal. If you really want to show it, simply add a "sensors" column. That object holds a collection of all the sensors in the application.

What other classes do you need here? The RunnableToIMonitorAdapter class implements the simple mapping between "run" and "monitor." The RunnableToIAssessAdapter class implements the simple mapping between "run" and "assess."

For the scenario itself, you need the following steps just to get things ready to go:

- The "sensors" object sends a message to the RunnableToIMonitorAdapter class to create a "monitor adapter" object (sending itself as a parameter).

- The "sensors" object sends a message to the Thread class to create a thread (sending a "monitor adapter" object as a parameter).

- The "sensors" object sends a message to the RunnableToIAssessAdapter class to create an "assess adapter" object (sending itself as a parameter).

- The "sensors" object sends a message to the Thread class to create another thread (sending an "assess adapter" object).

At this point, you're ready for business:

- The "sensors" object asks its "monitor sensors" thread to start.

- The "monitor sensors" object sends a "run" message to its "Runnable-to-IMonitor" adapter object.

- The "Runnable-to-IMonitor" object sends a "monitor all sensors" message to the "sensors" object.

And:

- The "sensors" object asks its "assess sensors" thread to start.

- The "assess sensors" object sends a "run" message to its "Runnable-to-IAssess adapter" object.

- The "Runnable-to-IAssess" object sends an "assess all sensors" message to the "sensors" object.

Figure 4-24 depicts the scenario view.

In Java, it looks like this:

```java
public interface IMonitor {
    void monitor(); }

public interface IAssess {
    void assess(); }

public class RunnableToIMonitorAdapter implements Runnable
{
✂
    // attributes / private / association
    private IMonitor myIMonitor;

    // methods / public / Runnable implementation
    public void run() {
        this.myIMonitor.monitor(); }
    // constructors
    public RunnableToIMonitorAdapter(IMonitor anIMonitor) {
        this.myIMonitor = anIMonitor ; }
✂
}

public class RunnableToIAssessAdapter implements Runnable {
✂
    // attributes / private / association
    private IAssess myIAssess;

    // methods / public / Runnable implementation
    public void run() {
        this.myIAssess.assess(); }

    // constructors
    public RunnableToIAssessAdapter(IAssess anIAssess) {
        this.myIAssess = anIAssess ; }
✂
}
```

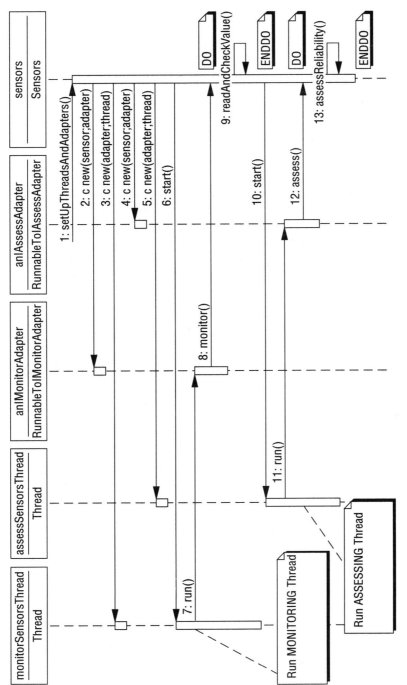

Figure 4-24. Monitoring and assessing threads, with corresponding interface adapters.

217

```
public class Sensors implements IMonitor, IAssess {

    // attributes / private / sensor collection
    private Vector sensorCollection = new Vector ();

    // attributes / private / threads
    private ResponsibleThread monitoringThread;
    private ResponsibleThread assessingThread;

    // attributes / private / interface adapters
    private RunnableToIMonitorAdapter myRunnableToIMonitorAdapter;
    private RunnableToIAssessAdapter myRunnableToIAssessAdapter;

    // methods / public / activation
    public void activate(int monitoringPriority, int assessingPriority) {
        // create the monitoring adapter and pass myself as the
        // parameter
        myRunnableToIMonitorAdapter = new
                RunnableToIMonitorAdapter(this);

        // create monitoring thread and pass the monitoring adapter as the
        // parameter
        this.monitoringThread = new ResponsibleThread
            (myRunnableToIMonitorAdapter);
        this.monitoringThread.setPriority(monitoringPriority);
        this.monitoringThread.start();

        // create the assessing adapter and pass myself as the
        // parameter
        myRunnableToIAssessAdapter = new
                RunnableToIAssessAdapter(this);

        // create monitoring thread and pass the assessing adapter as the
        // parameter
        this.assessingThread = new ResponsibleThread
            (myRunnableToIAssessAdapter);
        this.assessingThread.setPriority(assessingPriority);
        this.assessingThread.start(); }
```

```
// methods / public / IMonitor implementation
public void monitor() {
    for(;;) { // loop forever until thread is stopped
            this.readAndCheckValue();
            try {Thread.sleep(100);} catch(InterruptedException e){} } }

// methods / public / IAssess implementation
public void assess() {
    for(;;) { // loop forever until thread is stopped
            this.assessReliability();
            try {Thread.sleep(100);} catch(InterruptedException e){} } }

// methods / public / conducting business
public String checkStatus() {
    /* code goes here */ }

// methods / protected / conducting business
protected void readAndCheckValue() {
    /* code goes here.
        iterate through my sensor collection and
        ask each sensor to readAndCheckValue. */ }
protected void assessReliability() {
    /* code goes here.
        iterate through my sensor collection and
        ask each sensor to assessReliability. */ }

}
```

Code notes: The Zone remains the same. Sensors now implements the interfaces for two interface adapters and no longer implements the Runnable interface. The monitoring thread now enters through the IMonitor interface and the assessing thread now enters through the IAssess interface.*

---

*Java is strongly typed. All possible message-sends must be established at compile time. You cannot design with dynamic message dispatching (meaning, there is no mechanism like in C++ to create a pointer to a function and then de-reference that pointer [invoke the method it points to], and at any time reassign that pointer and then again de-reference that pointer [invoke the method it points to now]).

4.5   Summary

In this chapter, you've worked with threads, streams of program execution.

For an application to run, you must have at least one thread.

Why bother with multiple threads?

Most designs must account for multiple streams of program execution; this chapter shows how to do that safely.

Multiple threads let you give the appearance of doing more than one thing at a time. For example, your application can serve multiple clients at the same time.

Threads also give you the clean, simple way to design in the main thing you want your application to do, along with other things that you'd like it to be aware of or check on from time to time.

The strategies you learned and applied in this chapter are

Sync Access to Values Strategy: When multiple threads compete for values(s) within an object—and you try other thread paths but cannot avoid competition for these values—use sync'd methods to limit access (one thread at a time). For multithreaded objects, sync each method that compares, operates on, gets, or sets internal values.

Zoom In and Sync Strategy: Zoom in on exactly what you need to sync, factor it out into a separate method, and sync that method. Why? Sync for as little time as possible so other (potentially higher priority) threads waiting at the start of other sync methods for that object will get to run sooner rather than later.

Sync Access to Objects Strategy: When multiple threads compete for entry into each other's sync'd methods, use a gatekeeper to control access one thread at a time, and make sure the objects that the gatekeeper protects have no sync methods.

Value Gatekeeper Strategy: *Look for a method that increments or decrements a count of a limited resource. Sync that method; give it exclusive access to that count.*

Object Gatekeeper Strategy: *Look for a method that reserves or issues a limited resource, represented by the objects in that collection. Sync that method and give it exclusive access to that collection of objects.*

Four Thread Designs Strategy: *Apply these thread designs, looking for the simplest one that will satisfy your performance requirements. From simplest to most complex, consider: (1) single thread, (2) prioritized-object threads, (3) prioritized-method threads, (4) prioritized-method prioritized-object threads.*

Prioritized-Methods Strategy: *Prioritize your methods. Separate out cohesive functions with different priorities. Run higher priority methods in higher priority threads; run lower priority methods in lower priority threads.*

Thread Count Strategy: *Justify the existence of each thread in your design. If you can reduce the thread count and meet response time requirements, do so.*

Chapter 5

Design with Notification

This chapter explores three major notification mechanisms:

- passive: someone asks me if I've changed;
- timer-based: someone wakes me up; and
- active: a source notifies its listeners.

Passive notification is simple but resource intensive.

Timer-based notification is a useful pattern.

Active notification, with its many variations, is most interesting; it's an essential ingredient for problem–domain object reuse; it's an essential ingredient for designing loosely coupled subsystems. Java's early active notification mechanism (observable-observer) was a step in the right direction, but it had some problems. This chapter goes beyond that early weakness, showing you how to get the job done.

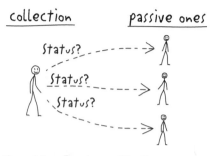

Figure 5-1.   Passive notification.

5.1 Passive Notification

Passive notification is the simplest of all notification mechanisms.

Passive notification is also known as polling. One object polls others, asking each one for its current status to see if it has changed in some meaningful way.

Perhaps you have a boss like this—always checking on you, always wondering how you are doing—in three words, a real pain (see Figure 5-1).

Figure 5-2 depicts a class diagram for passive notification.

As shown in the scenario in Figure 5-3, the corresponding object interactions are just what you'd expect.

Okay, let's apply this notification mechanism to Zoe's Zones (Figures 5-4 and 5-5).

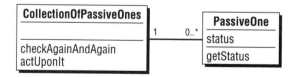

Figure 5-2.   A class diagram for passive notification.

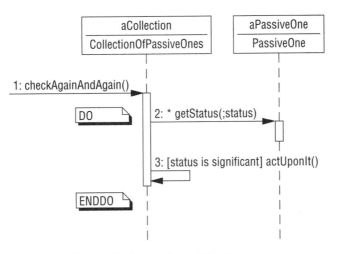

Figure 5-3. A scenario for passive notification.

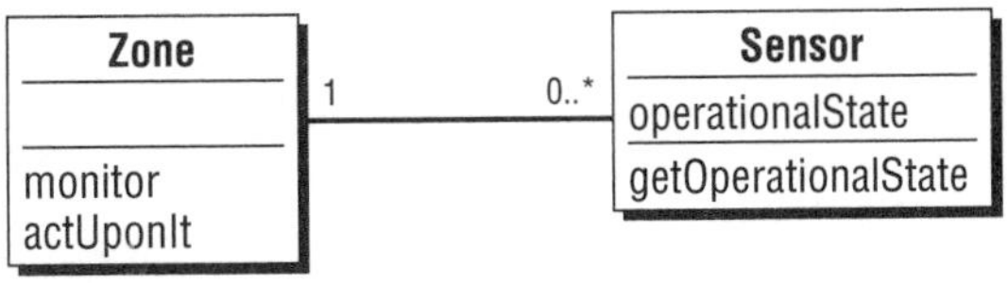

Figure 5-4. Passive notification for Zoe's Zones—class diagram.

The good news about passive notification is that it is simple.

The bad news is that passive notification is resource intensive in two ways: the loop itself and the number of objects that must be queried. Passive notification consumes resources asking about status even if the status never changes.

You can take care of the resource-intensive aspect of the loop itself by adding a timer (something we'll explore later in this chapter). However, the response time suffers. And if a problem occurs while you are sleeping, it might go undetected (depending on the problem domain you are working on).

When you have hundreds or thousands of objects to watch over (for example, the hundreds of items that might appear in a list within a UI), passive notification is still too awkward, and too slow.

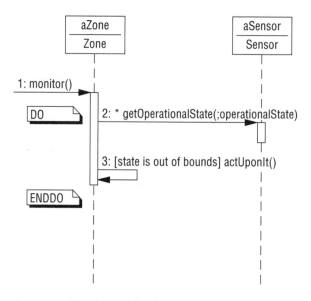

Figure 5-5.   Passive notification for Zoe's Zones—scenario.

5.2   Timer-Based Notification

Timer-based notification is another notification mechanism.

The idea behind a timer is simple: put a thread to sleep for a specified period of time, then let it wake up and continue.

5.2.1   Timer-Notification Pattern

The timer will sleep until a specified duration has passed. Figure 5-6 shows the class diagram.

Throughout this chapter, you'll need the following strategy:

Holder-Interface Strategy: *Establish a collection; define an interface.*

Figure 5-7 illustrates how that strategy fits in with the timer class diagram.

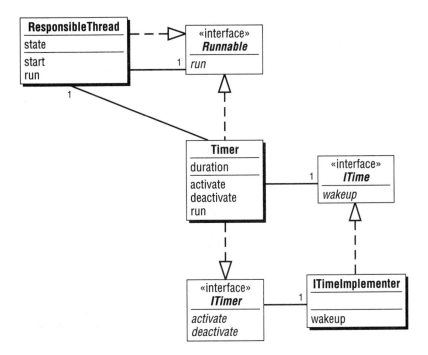

Figure 5-6.   Timer class diagram.

Figure 5-8 shows the timer scenario with a builder object to set up and activate a timer.

```
public interface ITimer {
    void activate(long duration);
    void deactivate(); }
```

```
public class Timer implements Runnable, ITimer {

    // attributes / private
    private long duration = 0;     // in milliseconds

    // attributes / private / associations
    private ITime myITime;
    private ResponsibleThread myThread;
    // methods / public / Runnable implementation
    public void run() {
        for (;;) { // continue sleep/wake-up cycle until thread is stopped
```

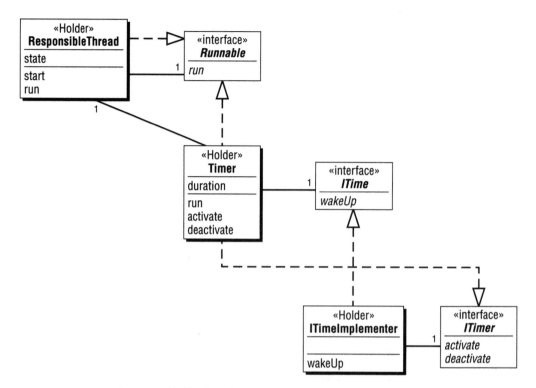

Figure 5-7. Holder-interface, again and again.

```
try {
   Thread.CurrentThread().sleep(this.duration);
} catch (InterruptedExecution e) {}
this.myITime.wakeup(); } }
```

Code notes: Sleep is a class method. So the code sends a message to the Thread class itself, asking it to put this thread to sleep.

```
// methods / public / ITimer implementation
public void activate(long aDuration) {
      // remember the duration
      this.duration = aDuration;
      // create and start a thread
      myThread = new ResponsibleThread(this);
      myThread.start(); }
```

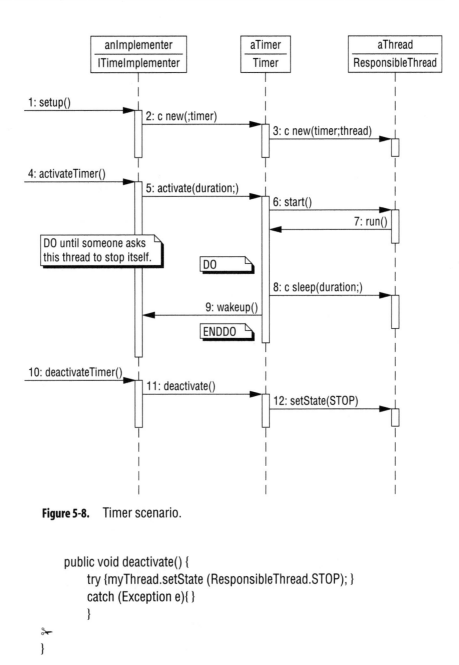

Figure 5-8. Timer scenario.

```
public void deactivate() {
    try {myThread.setState (ResponsibleThread.STOP); }
    catch (Exception e){ }
    }
✂
}

public class ITimeImplementer implements ITime {
✂
    // attributes / private
    private ITimer myITimer;
```

```
// methods / public / conducting business
public void setup() {
    this.myITimer = new Timer(); }

public void activateTimer() {
    this.myITimer.activate(3600000);   /* 1 hr = 3600000 milliseconds */ }

public void deactivateTimer() {
    this.myITimer.deactivate(); }
// methods / public / ITime implementation
public void wakeUp() {
    /* code goes here */ }

}
```

Code notes: This code puts the creation of the timer in the setup method and the activation of the timer in the activateTimer method. Alternatively, one could put both of these steps in the constructor of ITimeImplementer, to create and start a timer right away.

5.2.2   A Timer for Charlie's Charters

Suppose that once per day you need to generate a list of expiring reservations for each agent.

This requires timer(s) and low-priority thread(s).

You can design this in several ways:

- One thread, beginning with an "agents" object (a collection of all agents). The thread could wind its way from one agent to the next to the next, asking each one to build its own list of expiring reservations.

- One thread, beginning with an "agency" object (a collection of all reservations). The thread could wind its way through the reservations for that agency, building up a list of expiring reservations for each agent.

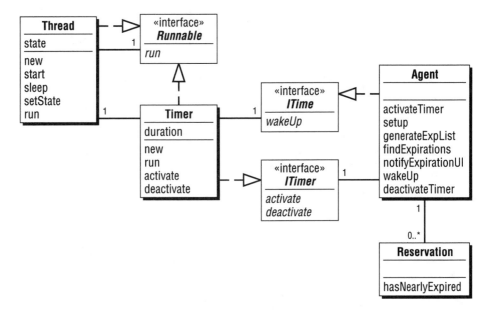

Figure 5-9. A timer for Charlie's Charters—class diagram.

- One thread per agent, each one beginning with an "agent" object. Each thread could wind its way through the reservations for that agent.

The "one thread per agent" approach has more low-priority threads, but it also points to a simpler overall design. Let's take a closer look.

Figure 5-9 depicts the class diagram.

Figure 5-10 shows the scenario.

In Java, it looks like this:

```
public class Agent implements ITime {

    // private / attributes
    private ITimer myITimer;
```

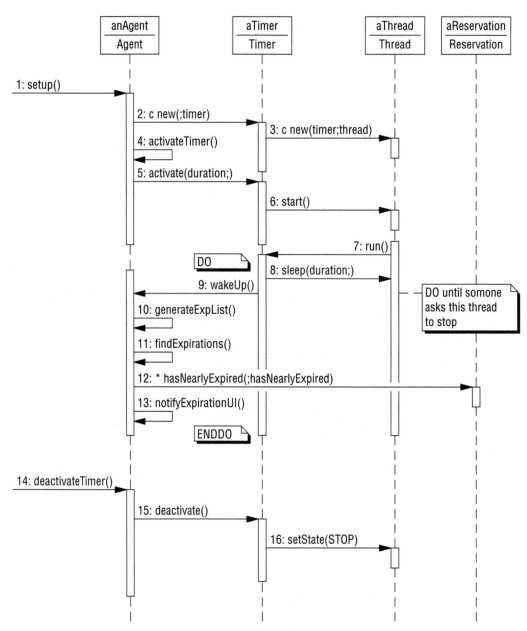

Figure 5-10. A timer for Charlie's Charters—scenario.

```
// methods / public / conducting business
public void setup() {
    this.myITimer = new Timer(); }

public void activateTimer() {
    this.myITimer.activate(86400000);        /* 24 hr */ }

public void deactivateTimer() {
    this.myITimer.deactivate(); }

// methods / public / ITime implementation
public void wakeUp() {
    /* - generate expiration list
       - find expirations
       - notify expiration UI */ }

}
```

Code notes: This code sets the timer to wake up every 24 hours. When the agent object is told to wake up, it generates a list of expiring reservations and notifies the appropriate UI component.

5.3   Active Notification

Active notification puts the notification responsibility within the object that changes. That object takes action.

Hmmm. Sounds much more like an object-oriented approach: I change; I let others (who have registered interest in me) know that I've changed.

One can summarize active notification in two words: source-listener.

Take a closer look at source-listener and significant variations on that theme:

- Observable-observer

- Source-listener (itself)

- Source-support-listener

  (JavaBeans-style notification)

- Producer-bus-consumer

  (InfoBus-style notification)

- Model-view-controller

  (Swing-style notification)

- Source-distributed listener

  (Enterprise JavaBeans-style notification)

5.3.1 Observable-Observer

Observable-observer is an object-model pattern. It is also known as publisher-subscriber, model-view, and document-view (Figure 5-11).

Here's how it works.

First, someone tells an observable who its observers are:

- Some object (let's call it a builder) asks an observable to add an observer.

- An observable adds that observer to its list of observers.

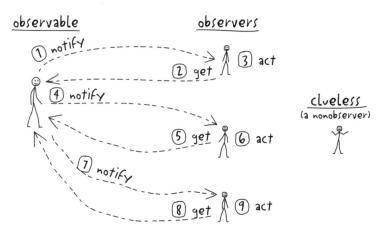

Figure 5-11. An observable and its observers.

Then, an observable notifies its observers:

- When an observable object changes itself in a significant way (meaning, in a way that someone else might be interested in), it notifies each of its observers.

Finally, each observer does its thing:

- Each observer gets whatever it needs.
- Each observer takes whatever action it deems appropriate.

Are there lots of messages? Actually, compared with passive notification:

- Observable-observer *reduces* overall message traffic.
- Observable-observer *reduces* the coupling that an observable has with its observers.

Let's consider the point about reduced coupling.

Observable-observer lets you put together PD and UI objects in such a way that PD objects know very, very little about UI objects. PD objects are not hopelessly devoted to UI objects, which is a very good thing. Observable-observer facilitates reuse of PD objects.

In a similar vein, observable-observer lets you put together a subsystem with other, supporting subsystems. A subsystem knows very, very little about the supporting subsystems. That subsystem no longer has a fatal attraction to its supporting subsystems. Observable-observer facilitates reuse of a subsystem (loose coupling); at the same time, it facilitates extensibility as well (easy to add, change, or remove supporting subsystems, as needed).

Okay, then. So how might we model (and ultimately implement) something called observable-observer? Classes and inheritance? Or composition and interfaces?

Several options are possible.

Balanced Design Strategy: Design at two extremes and then some-where in between. Design connotes looking at alternatives and picking a reasonable approach.

Let's first consider the extremes and then the middle ground.

5.3.1.1 A Pair of Classes (One Extreme)

One extreme is a pair of classes, with or without inheritance.

Without inheritance, we'd need to design and build both observable and observer into the classes that needed them, each and every time, from scratch (Figure 5-12).

Sounds like too much work. We can do better than that.

Some methods remain the same:

> addObserver—adds an object to a list of observers

> deleteObserver—deletes an object from a list of observers

> deleteObservers—deletes *all* observers from a list of observers

> notifyObservers—sends an "update" message to each observer, letting it know about a change that has taken place

Yet some methods must be customized for a specific observable and its observers:

Observable

- changeState—do something significant, something worth notifying the observers about

- getStatus—get the value(s) requested by an observer, something it needs to ask, upon notification that what it is watching (the observable) has changed in some way.

Observer

- update—initiate an observer's response to a notification from an observable

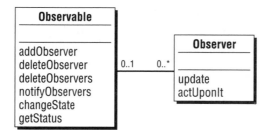

Figure 5-12. A pair of classes.

- actUponIt—upon notification, this is the action that each observer takes

Some methods remain the same; some methods must be customized.

This sounds like a good opportunity for inheritance, showing what is the same (superclass) and what is different (subclasses).

But is this a good idea (remember Chapter 2, Design with Composition, Rather than Inheritance)? Let's evaluate this, in the pages ahead. For now, though, we're in the midst of considering an extreme: a classes-only approach.

Let's try it out. Figure 5-13 shows the class diagram.

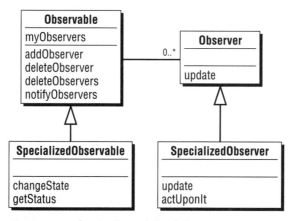

Figure 5-13. A pair of specialized classes.

A SpecializedObservable class needs its own method name for changeState and getStatus. It also needs its own implementation for those methods.

A SpecializedObserver class needs its own method name for actUponIt, and it needs its own implementation for it.

But what about the update method? It's listed in both Observer and SpecializedObserver. In a class diagram, seeing a method name appear in a class and a subclass indicates that

- the superclass establishes that the method signature must be implemented by all of its specialization classes, or

- the superclass establishes a method signature and some common capability, and now a subclass is extending that common capability.

What about in this case? The Observer class has an update method. There is no implementation behind it; every "update" method is something you must work out for each subclass of Observer. No implementation? That sounds exactly like what an interface is all about: an interface is a list of one or more method signatures—no implementation. Just method signatures, no implementation: that's a good hint that you should be using an interface here.

Extracting Interfaces from a Class Hierarchy Strategy: *When you find that a subclass is inheriting one or more methods that are merely method signatures, use an interface for those method signatures. (That's exactly what an interface is for.)*

Let's also take a look at the corresponding scenario (Figure 5-14).

Consider the parameters for the update method.

The first parameter tells the observer object whom it needs to be talking to, and it obviates the need for an observer to keep a list of its observables. So including the first parameter simplifies an observer: there is one less collection to maintain.

The second parameter tells the observer what kind of change has occurred, and it obviates the need for an observer to ask for every

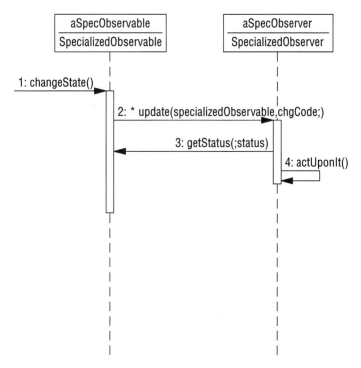

Figure 5-14. Interactions for objects in a pair of specialized classes.

status-related attribute in each observable, hoping to find out what has indeed changed. So including the second parameter simplifies an observer's job, reducing the number of interactions between an observer and each of its observables.

5.3.1.2 A Pair of Interfaces (Another Extreme)

Let's continue to be extremists, at least for a while longer.

Interfaces are cool. How about a solution made up entirely of interfaces? (Figure 5-15)

But wait a minute. You can't draw something like that—it makes a promise that we can't keep. You see, an interface can't be required to hold a collection of objects.

Figure 5-15.   An interfaces–only class diagram (not allowed in Java).

An interface is simply a collection of method signatures, no more, no less.

Can an interface imply that an implementer might hold some number of other objects?

Yes, with some agreed-upon naming conventions, you could imply attributes (get, set) and associations (add, remove). Still, you cannot require an implementer of that interface to build it that way. Remember, an interface is a collection of method signatures— that's all.

Here, you need more than just interfaces; interfaces are not enough, when it comes to building an effective object model. You also need classes that implement those interfaces.

5.3.1.3   Classes and An Interface (Standing on Shaky Ground)

Go for the middle ground: inheritance for observables, interfaces for observers.

In fact, Java includes an Observable class and an Observer interface.

In other words, Observable has implementation and interface we can inherit; Observer defines an interface we can implement.

The middle ground looks something like Figure 5-16.

From the model in Figure 5-16, we see that a specialized observable object knows some number of observers (objects in classes that implement the Observer interface, that is). That makes good sense.

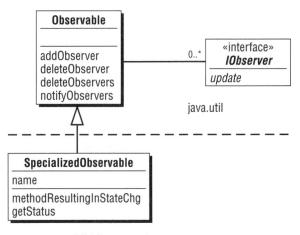

Figure 5-16. Middle ground.

The part above the dashed line comes from the *java.util* class library; the part below the dashed line is what you design and build.

5.3.1.4 Java's Observable Class?

Is it really such a good idea to inherit from Observable? Is this really the way to go on this?

Check it out.

Each time you have a new kind of observable, you must add a new specialized observable class and new classes that implement the corresponding observer interfaces.

For example, suppose you add a specialization of Observable, called Person. If PersonObservable includes name and address, then you would add:

- A specialized observable class (Person)

    with getName and setName methods

- An observer interface for name (IName)

- An observer interface for address (IAddress)

You could reuse the interfaces, as long as the parameter lists for the method signatures are not hardwired back to objects in a specific class (such as PersonObservable, for example).

Yet is Observable, specializing into Person, really a valid use of inheritance? Apply the strategy from Chapter 2, Design with Composition Rather than Inheritance.

When to Inherit Strategy: Inheritance is used to extend attributes and methods, but encapsulation is weak within a class hierarchy, so use of this mechanism is limited. Use it when you can satisfy the following criteria:

1. *"Is a special kind of," not "is a role played by a"*
2. *Never needs to transmute to be an object in some other class*
3. *Extends rather than overrides or nullifies*
4. *Does not subclass what is merely a utility class*
5. *Within PD: Expresses special kinds of roles, transactions, or things.*

Person, if made a subclass of Observable, would subclass what is merely a utility class. Not a good idea.

Hence, you really ought to use composition here, rather than inheritance. Why? Composition is easier to change, easier to add to existing classes, and it's easier when it comes to providing several flavors of that functionality (should the need arise).

Should you inherit from Java's Observable class? The answer is no. Java's Observable class is not very useful. An ObservableComponent class would be far better (that's something we'll consider further in the pages ahead).

5.3.1.5 Java's Observer Interface?

Java has an Observer interface. It looks like this:

```
public interface Observer {
    void update(Observable observed, Object argument); }
```

At this point you could (1) build your own ObservableComponent class, so you can use observable components whenever you want to by using composition (rather than inheritance), and (2) use a corresponding Observer interface.

Can you use Java's Observer interface? Or do we need to define one of our own?

Take a closer look at that interface declaration, specifically at the parameter:

```
Observable observed
```

The designer of this Java interface severely limited its usefulness by specifying that the interface should work with objects in the class Observable or its subclasses, rather than allowing for objects from Object or its subclasses, such as:

```
Object observed
```

Java's Observer interface assumes that it only needs to work with objects that are in the Observable class or its subclasses. Hmmm. That's not good news; we've already seen that inheriting from Observable is not the way to go.

In fact, you cannot use Java's Observer interface in this design. Why? That interface assumes that it works only with objects in the class Observable or its subclasses. But you need an interface that will work with objects from our own ObservableComponent class.

Can you use Java's Observer interface? No. In fact, its design weakness inspired the following strategy:

Don't Limit Your Interfaces with Needless Assumptions Strategy: *Consider typing your interface parameters as a built-in type (for example: int, float, String, StringBuffer, Object). Let each implementer of that interface test for the specific classes of objects it works with. Reason why: to increase the likelihood of reuse of each interface.*

How do you overcome this problem? You simply introduce a very similar, but more general interface, called IObserver:

```
public interface IObserver {
    void update(Object observed, Object argument); }
```

5.3.1.6 Composition and Interfaces (to the Rescue)

Composition and interfaces are an awesome combination!

Actually, you saw this "composition and interface" dynamic duo earlier in this book, in Chapter 3, Design with Interfaces, with:

- DateReserveUI—a *composition* of objects it interacts with
- IDateReserve—a corresponding *interface* implemented by the classes corresponding to the objects that DateReserveUI is composed of

Yes, you did *add in* capability by building the composition and implementing the promised interface. The composition object ends up with some "added-in" capabilities.*

It's now time to apply both ObservableComponent and IObserver.

Figure 5-17 is an informal sketch of this application.

Figure 5-18 presents the class diagram.

---

*The same design approach may be applied when building C++ apps. You can dedicate part of your class hierarchies to expressing interfaces, namely, C++ classes that consist only of method signatures. On the other hand, when designing C++ apps, you can also "mix in" behaviors from multiple superclasses; however, the ever-decreasing amount of encapsulation within a class hierarchy with multiple-inheritance behavior makes this an unwieldy approach (something to avoid, when possible).

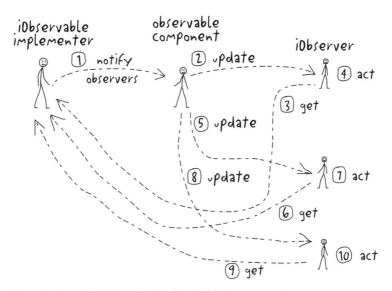

Figure 5-17. Working with an observable component.

```
        «interface»
        IObservable
    addIObserver
    deleteIObserver
    deleteIObservers
```

```
  IObservableImplementer                    ObservableComponent
                              1
    addIObserver                         addIObserver
    deleteIObserver                      deleteIObserver
    deleteIObservers                     deleteIObservers
                                         notifyIObservers
```

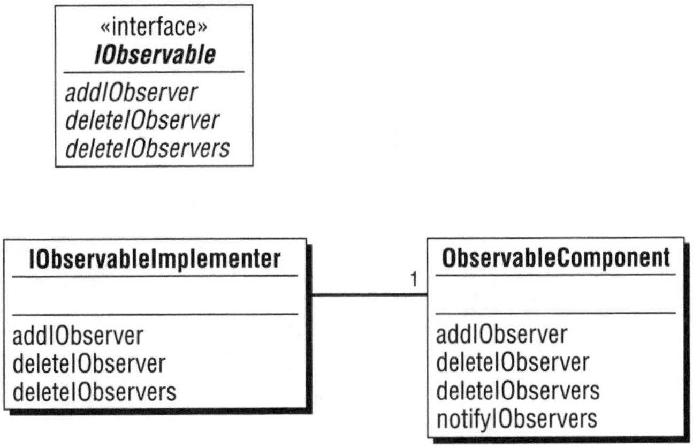

Figure 5-18. Using an observable component.

A scenario is depicted next (Figure 5-19). Note that in the scenario:

- A builder object sets up an observable and its observers.

- A sender object sends a message to an observable, resulting in something of significance happening in the observable.

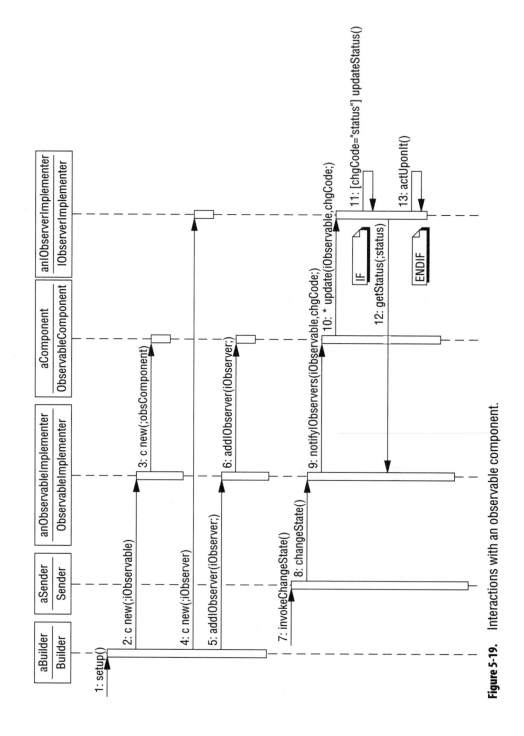

Figure 5-19. Interactions with an observable component.

Here is what happens:

- When an observable has a state change, it sends a message to its own observable component object.
- For each of its observers, that observable component object,

  Sends an update message to an observer.

Then each observer

- Evaluates the change code from that observer;
- Sends messages to get whatever it needs; and
- Acts upon it.

In Java, it looks like this:

```java
public interface IObserver {
    void update(Object theObserved, Object changeCode); }

public interface IObservable {
    void addIObserver(IObserver anIObserver);
    void deleteIObserver(IObserver anIObserver);
    void deleteIObservers(); }

public class ObservableComponent {

    // attributes / private / associations
    private Vector myIObservers = new Vector();

    // methods / public / accessors for association values
    public void addIObserver(IObserver anIObserver) {
        this.myIObservers.addElement(anIObserver); }

    public void deleteIObserver(IObserver anIObserver) {
        this.myIObservers.removeElement(anIObserver); }

    public void deleteIObservers() {
        this.myIObservers.removeAllElements(); }
```

```java
// methods / public / notification
public void notifyIObservers(Object theObserved, Object changeCode) {
    // iterate through the vector of IObservers and
    // tell each IObserver to update
    Enumeration myIObserversList = this.myIObservers.elements();
    while (myIObserversList.hasMoreElements()) {
        // must cast the element to IObserver
        IObserver anIObserver =
                (IObserver) myIObserversList.nextElement();
        anIObserver.update(theObserved, changeCode); } }
}


public class IObserverImplementer implements IObserver {

    // methods / public / IObserver implementation
    public void update(Object theObserved, Object changeCode) {
        if (changeCode instanceof String) {
            String theChangeCode = (String)changeCode;
            /* if theChangeCode is the one I'm looking for,
               then get the status from theObserved */ } }

}


public class IObservableImplementer implements IObservable {

    // attributes / private
    private int state;                   // something that represents my state

    // attributes / private / associations
    private ObservableComponent myObservableComponent =
            new ObservableComponent();

    // methods / public / IObservable implementation
    public void addIObserver(IObserver anIObserver) {
        this.myObservableComponent.addIObserver(anIObserver); }

    public void deleteIObserver(IObserver anIObserver) {
        this.myObservableComponent.deleteIObserver(anIObserver); }
```

```
        public void deleteIObservers() {
            this.myObservableComponent.deleteIObservers(); }

        // methods / public / resulting in a state change
        public void changeState(int newState) {
            this.state = newState;
            // instruct my observable component to notify the IObservers
            // pass myself as the observed and "state" as the change code
            this.myObservableComponent.notifyIObservers(this, "state"); }
```

✂
```
}
```

Code notes: The Builder in the previous scenario can be just about any object that builds the relationships between an IObservableImplementer object and its IObserverImplementer objects.

5.3.1.7 PD-to-UI Notification for Charlie's Charters

Apply the "observable component–IObserver interface" pattern to Charlie's Charters and its flight descriptions.

When should you message and when should you notify?

Message Inward, Notify Outward Strategy:

UI-invoked changes: message inward from UI to PD.

PD-invoked changes: notify outward from PD to UI.

Consider what happens when the state of a flight description changes. For example, if the departureTime changes, any UI observers of that flight description should be notified, so the UI observers can update themselves accordingly.

Apply the "observable component–IObserver interface" pattern, (Figure 5-20).

The flight-description class is application specific. The DateReserveUI is something that can be reused in an analogous (in this case, date reserving) application. And the ObservableComponent class is reused as is (it stays the same, for any application).

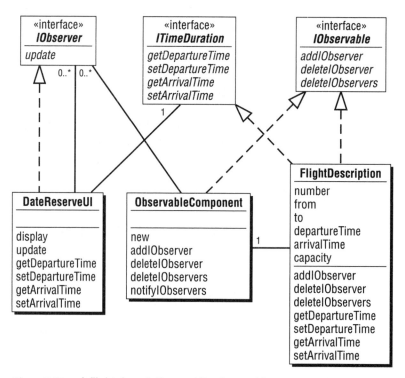

Figure 5-20.   A flight description and its observable component.

A scenario? It needs a builder object to set things up. It needs a sender object, representing some PD object or a UI object that sends a setFrom message. Then it's ready to roll (Figure 5-21).

In Java, it looks like this:

```
public interface ITimeDuration {
    Date getDepartureTime();
    void setDepartureTime(Date aTime);
    Date getArrivalTime();
    void setArrivalTime(Date aTime); }
```

Code notes: The Date class includes both dates and times.

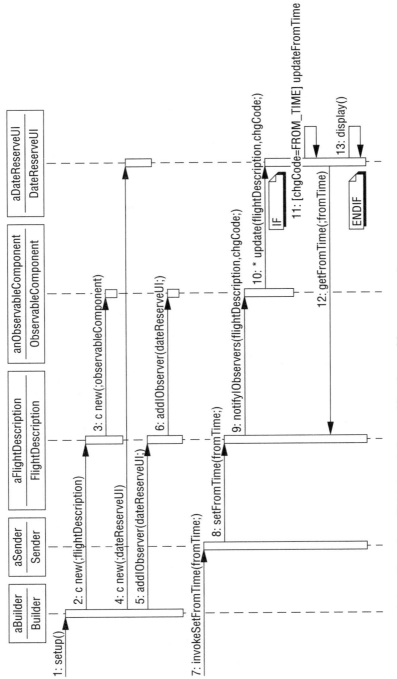

Figure 5-21. Interactions for a flight description and its observable component.

```
public class FlightDescription implements ITimeDuration {

    // attributes / private
    private Date departureTime;
    private Date arrivalTime;

    // attributes / private / associations
    private ObservableComponent myObservableComponent =
            new ObservableComponent();

    // methods / public / ITimeDuration implementation
    public Date getDepartureTime() {
        return this.departureTime; }

    public void setDepartureTime(Date aTime) {
        this.departureTime = aTime;
        // tell my observable component to notify the IObservers
        this.myObservableComponent.notifyIObservers(
            this, "departureTime"); }
    public Date getArrivalTime() {
        return this.arrivalTime; }

    public void setArrivalTime(Date aTime) {
        this.arrivalTime = aTime;
        // tell my observable component to notify the IObservers
        this.myObservableComponent.notifyIObservers(this, "arrivalTime"); }

}

public class DateReserveUI  implements IObserver {

    // methods / public / IObserver implementation
    public void update(Object theObserved, Object changeCode) {
        // make sure the change code is a string
        if (changeCode instanceof String) {
            String theChangeCode = (String)changeCode;

            // check to see if the correct change code
            if (theChangeCode.equalsIgnoreCase("departureTime")) {
```

```
                    // make sure the observed is an ITimeDuration
                    if (theObserved instanceof ITimeDuration) {
                            ITimeDuration anITimeDuration =
                                    (ITimeDuration)theObserved;

                            // get the new departure time from the iTimeDuration
                            Date newDepartureTime =
                                    anITimeDuration.getDepartureTime();
                            /* update the UI with the new departure time */ } } } }
    ✂
    }
```

Code notes: This code uses three nested if statements in the update method. It can be written as three separate "if" statements that immediately return from the method if a condition is *not* met. The code makes these types of checks just to be on the safe side.

ObservableComponent is the same code as the previous example.

So, just how important is the "observable component–IObserver" pattern?

Without it, you'd be stuck with

- UI objects that continuously poll for changes (acceptable only for the simplest of UIs), or

- PD objects that are hardwired to UI objects, prohibiting any meaningful reuse of PD objects—within this application or in subsequent applications.

Now let's consider a variation on this theme: repeaters.

5.3.1.8 Observable Component–Repeater Pattern

A repeater takes a message as is, verbatim, and sends it along to potentially some number of objects.

So what is a repeater? A repeater first acts as an observer; then it passes along the news, as an observable (Figure 5-22).

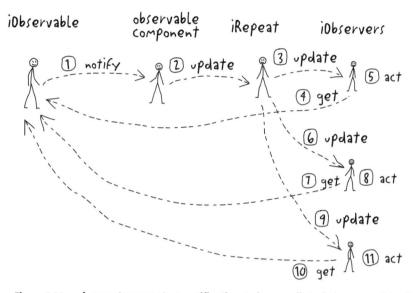

Figure 5-22. A repeater repeats a notification to its own list of observers (single thread).

Why use a repeater? If you want to change from one observer to another and yet continue to use the same list of observers, a repeater makes that change much simpler (Figure 5-23).

Here's the strategy:

Repeater Strategy: *Use a repeater when you need to build a standard list of observers, so you can change observables and still use that standard list as is.*

You already have an IObservable interface. Now you need an IRepeat interface, a combination of both IObservable and IObserver interfaces. The resulting class diagram is shown in Figure 5-24.

A scenario? Well, you'll need two sections:

- Setup

    Add an iRepeat object and an iObserver object to an iObservable object.

- Notification

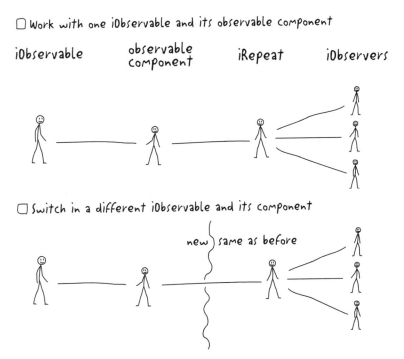

Figure 5-23. The motivation for using a repeater.

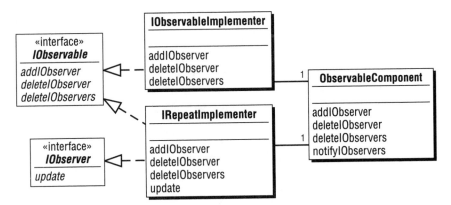

Figure 5-24. A repeater is a combination of both observable and observer.

An iObservable notifies its iRepeat objects.

Each iRepeat object notifies its iObserver objects.

Each iObserver object gets what it needs from its iObservable.

Each iObserver acts accordingly.

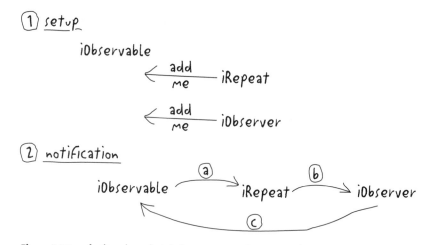

Figure 5-25. A planning sketch for an upcoming scenario.

Sometimes it's helpful to begin with a preliminary scenario sketch, before working out dynamics in detail with a scenario view. Figure 5-25 is such a sketch.

Figure 5-26 shows the scenario view itself.

In Java, it looks like this:

```
public interface IRepeat extends IObservable, IObserver {}

public class IRepeatImplementer implements IRepeat {

    // attributes / private / associations
    private ObservableComponent myObservableComponent =
        new ObservableComponent();

    // methods / public / IRepeat implementation
    public void addIObserver(IObserver anIObserver) {
        this.myObservableComponent.addIObserver(anIObserver); }

    public void deleteIObserver(IObserver anIObserver) {
        this.myObservableComponent.deleteIObserver(anIObserver); }
```

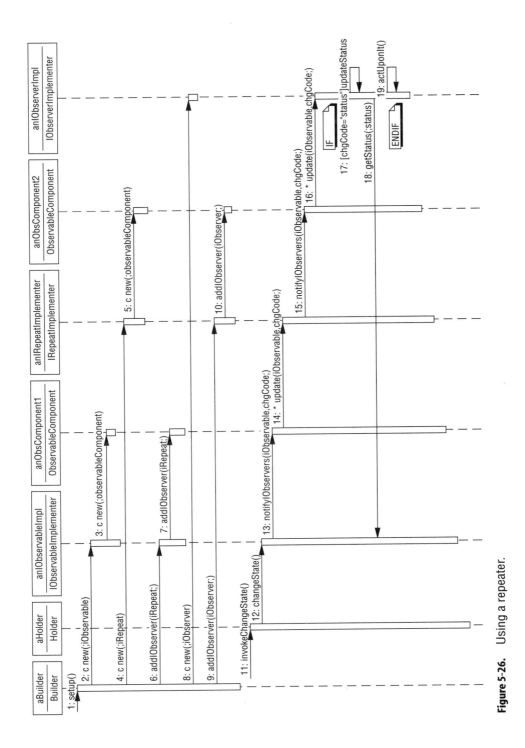

Figure 5-26. Using a repeater.

257

```
public void deletelObservers() {
    this.myObservableComponent.deletelObservers(); }

public void update(Object theObserved, Object changeCode) {
    // my update is to notify my iObservers with these parameters
    this.myObservableComponent.notifylObservers(
        theObserved, changeCode); }

}
```

Code notes: This code could use a generic name for this class like Repeater. An IRepeatImplementer object behaves like a component since it just passes along the update parameters to its own ObservableComponent object.

5.3.1.9 Threaded-Observable Component

So far, you've been working with a single-thread solution, as shown in Figure 5-27.

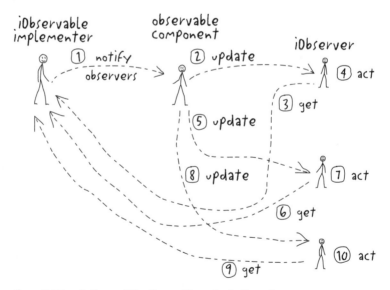

Figure 5-27. Active notification, with a single thread.

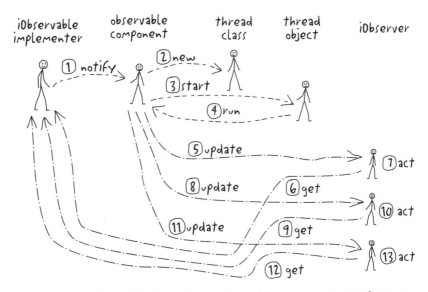

Figure 5-28. Active notification with an observable component spawning a separate notification thread.

However you could run notification on a different thread

- at a lower priority if the thread running through iObservable is more important, or

- at a higher priority if the thread running through iObservers is more important.

Figure 5-28 shows what this might look like.

The notification thread can run as long as it needs to as long as it has updates to take care of. When no more updates are pending, then an observable component can ask the notification thread to stop itself.

It's time for a class diagram—this time with a threaded-observable component (Figure 5-29).

The scenario in Figure 5-30 includes: (1) setup, (2) an observable thread, and (3) a notification thread. Check it out.

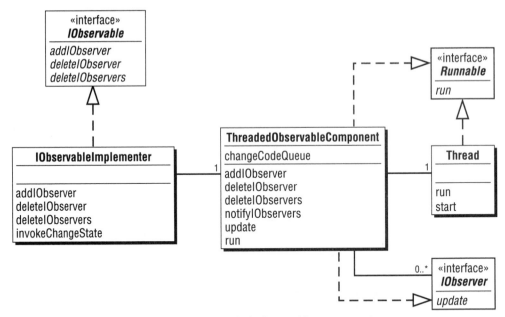

Figure 5-29. Adding a threaded-observable component.

So far, so good. But what happens when a single threaded-observable component receives another notifyIObservers message even before the first one is done?

- The notification thread keeps on running through its lists of iObservers.

- The threaded observable component queues up additional notification requests (meaning, it queues up the change codes that come in).

- The notification thread, once it's made it through its list of iObservers, grabs the next notification request from the queue, and begins another pass through its list of iObservables.

- Eventually, the notification thread comes back and finds that the queue is empty. At that point, the observable component asks the notification thread to stop.

- Upon arrival of a notifyIObservers message, the whole thing begins anew.

Figure 5-31 offers a more detailed look at a threaded-observable component in a class diagram.

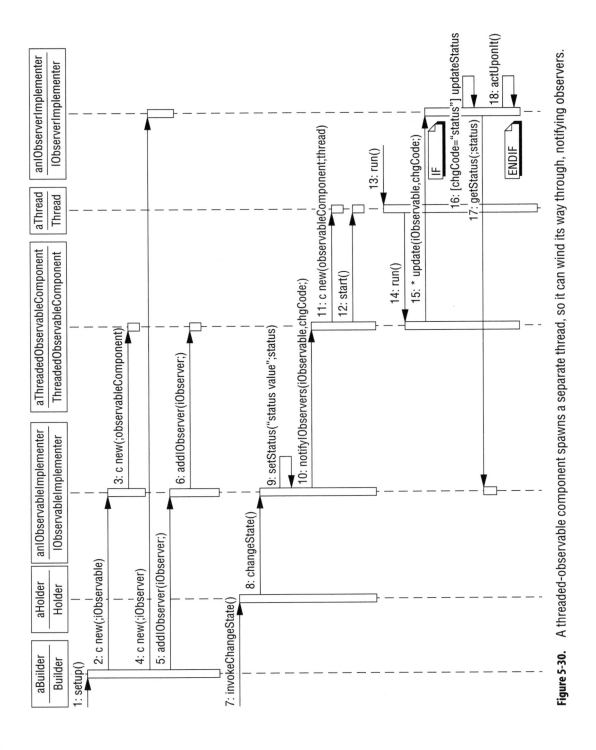

Figure 5-30. A threaded-observable component spawns a separate thread, so it can wind its way through, notifying observers.

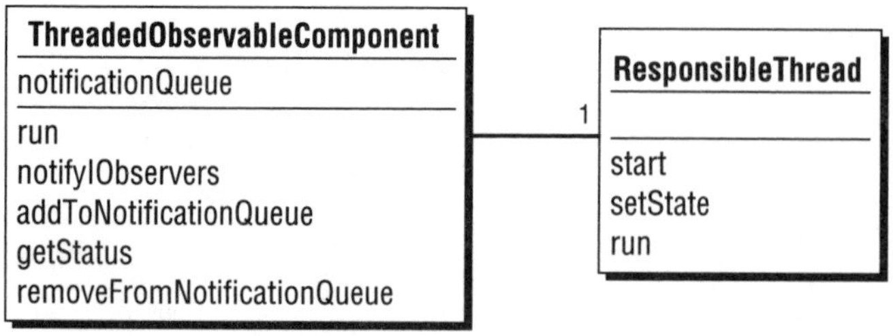

Figure 5-31.   A more detailed look at a threaded-observable component.

The details of working with a notification queue are spelled out in the following scenario shown in Figure 5-32.

Take a closer look at the sync blocks in Figure 5-32. The first sync makes sure that just one notification thread is spawned. The second sync makes sure that the observable thread, which at some point invokes setStatus, is kept from interfering while the notification thread runs through getStatus. The third sync makes sure that we can stop a notification thread without some other thread getting in and adding a notification request at the same time.

What about the rest of the design? Well, yes, anyone that accesses the status attribute needs to use a sync, to ensure thread-safe access. That about does it.

In Java, it looks like this:

```
public class ThreadedObservableComponent implements Runnable {

    // attributes / private
    private Vector notificationQueue = new Vector();

    // attributes / private / associations
    private Vector myIObservers = new Vector();
    private ResponsibleThread notificationThread;

    // methods / public / notification
    public void notifyIObservers(Object theObserved, Object changeCode) {
        this.addToNotificationQueue(theObserved, changeCode); }
```

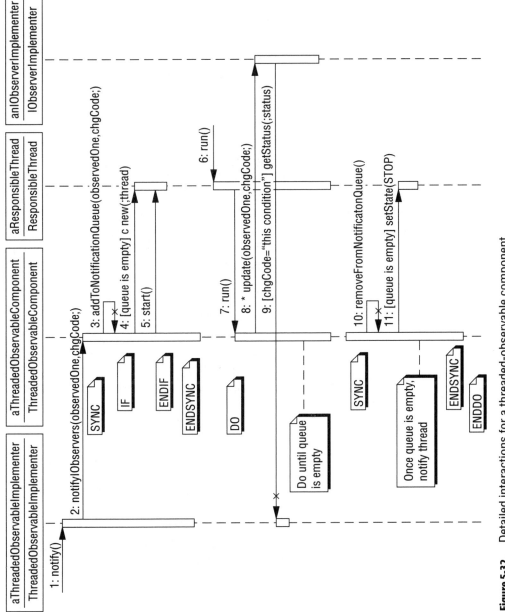

Figure 5-32. Detailed interactions for a threaded-observable component.

```java
// methods / public / Runnable implementation
public void run() {
    do { // while the notification queue is not empty
        // get the observed and the change code from the
        // notification queue
        Object theObserved = this.notificationQueue.elementAt(0);
        Object changeCode = this.notificationQueue.elementAt(1);
        // iterate through the vector of IObservers and tell
        // each IObserver to update
        Enumeration myIObserversList = this.myIObservers.elements();
        while (myIObserversList.hasMoreElements()) {
          // must cast the element to IObserver
          IObserver anIObserver = (IObserver)
                  myIObserversList.nextElement();
          anIObserver.update(theObserved, changeCode); } }
    while (this.removeFromNotificationQueue()); }
// methods / protected / synchronized
protected synchronized
    void addToNotificationQueue(Object theObserved,
                  Object changeCode) {
        this.notificationQueue.addElement(theObserved);
        this.notificationQueue.addElement(changeCode);
        if (this.notificationQueue.size() == 2) {
                // the queue was empty so create and start a thread
                this.notificationThread = new ResponsibleThread(this);
                this.notificationThread.start(); } }

protected synchronized
    boolean removeFromNotificationQueue() {
        // remove first two elements from the notification queue
        this.notificationQueue.removeElementAt(0);
        this.notificationQueue.removeElementAt(0);
        if (this.notificationQueue.size() == 0) {
          // the queue is empty so ask the thread to stop itself.
          try {this.notificationThread.setState(ResponsibleThread.STOP);}
          catch (Exception e) {}
          return false; /* queue is empty so return false */ }
        return true; /* queue is not empty so return true */ }

}
```

Code notes: There are many ways to implement the notification queue. This code uses a vector so that you can add new notifications to the end of the queue and can remove old notifications from the beginning of the queue.

5.3.2 Source-Listener

JDK 1.1 introduced event sources and event listeners. Consider the sketch in Figure 5-33.

This looks rather familiar, doesn't it? It's just like the sketch for observable-observer from earlier in this chapter. So what's the difference that you get with source-listener? The design is slightly different. And what you supply is slightly different. Take a look at the designs, side-by-side (Figure 5-34).

That which is above the dashed line comes from the *java.util* class library; that which is below the dashed line is what you design and build.

You've already seen the design on the left. Now take a look at the design on the right. The design within *java.util* is fairly spartan.

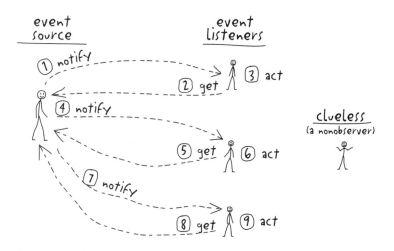

Figure 5-33. An event source and some event listeners.

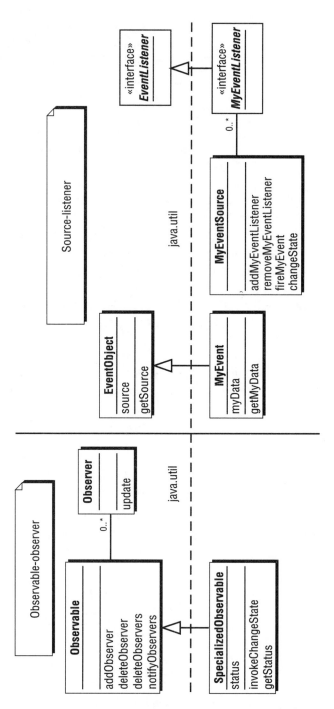

Figure 5-34. Comparing observable-observer and source-listener.

EventObject is an abstract class. The getSource method is defined (ask an event object for its source and it will tell you). The design requires you to inherit from EventObject, defining your own event class and corresponding event objects. By convention, the name for EventObject subclasses ends with the word "Event."

Now check out that interface on the right. Hmmm. The EventListener interface has absolutely no method signatures in it (gee, how helpful!). Actually, the interface is included as a grouping mechanism for whatever event listeners you might define; your event listener extends the EventListener interface and then establishes the method signatures you need.

Bottom line: the design within *java.util* requires you to do most of the work: you specialize your own event object, you design and build your own notification mechanism for your event source; and you design and implement your own event listener interface.

Okay, so now compare and contrast the two designs. Observable-observer uses inheritance of the notification mechanism. In that design, you are stuck with whatever notification mechanism it provides; there is no possibility of plugging in another one.

Event-listener uses inheritance for kinds of events. You are responsible for providing your own notification mechanism and in fact you could use composition and plug in the notification algorithm of your choice (for example: FIFO, LIFO, or prioritized by kind of event). The good news is added flexibility. The bad news is that you have to build it yourself.

Following the same basic pattern as observable-observer, the scenario for the newer design looks like Figure 5-35.

So an object in an app, acting as a builder, creates an event source and an event listener, and asks the event source to add that event listener to its notification list. Then, whenever that event source changes in a way it deems significant, it notifies all of the listeners on its list.

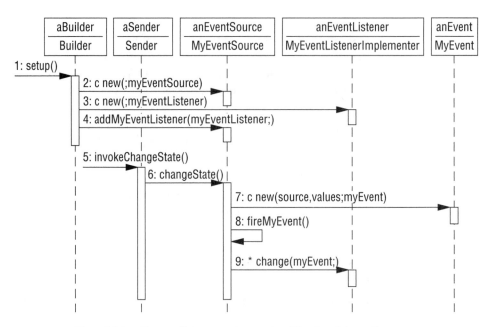

Figure 5-35.   Source-listener: setup and notification interactions.

Here's a Java snippet for an event source notifying its listeners:

```
public class MyEventSource {
✂
   private Vector myEventListeners; /*created by constructor*/
   public void fireMyEvent() {
     MyEvent myEvent = new MyEvent(); /*then initialize it*/
     Vector copyMyEventListeners = (Vector) this.myEventListeners.clone();
     Enumeration myEventListenerList = copyMyEventListeners.elements();
     while (myEventListenerList.hasMoreElements()) {
       MyEventListener myEventListener =
         (MyEventListener) myEventListenerList.nextElement();
       myEventListener.change(myEvent);  }
   }
✂
}
```

Note that the event source makes a clone of the list, its very own copy. This is the norm in notification mechanisms: take a snapshot of the current notification, then notify everyone on that list. The idea behind the snapshot is to capture the state of the notification list right at the moment an event source detects a need to notify its listeners about something; every listener who is "signed up" at that point should hear the news.

5.3.3 Source-Support-Listener (JavaBeans-Style Notification)

Source-support-listener is the fundamental notification for JavaBean interaction. It's not the most effective mechanism, just the fundamental one.

You see, JavaBeans are components. To be useful, components need to become aware of each other and talk with each other.

You can design collaborative beans with case-by-case, specific interfaces, protocols and data content. That's what source-support-listener is all about.

Or you can design collaborative beans using standard interfaces and protocols, with specific data content. That's what producer-bus-consumer goes after (see the next section in this chapter).

JavaBeans that are loaded from the same class loader can find and interact with each other. Beans sign up with each other, notify each other, and then interpret the content of each notification. Beans ask each other questions at design time, mainly to verify that methods that one bean plans to invoke are indeed implemented by another bean. This "question asking" is called *introspection* (pretty cool, huh?). Still, even with introspection taking place, you need to think things through in advance and:

- Design who participates in a notification mechanism.

- Design what gets passed in a notification.

- Design what gets done with the content received in a notification.

Yes, it's true: you need to design the specific contexts in which you can use any software Integrated Circuit (IC). We need those ICs, absolutely. Yet we also need well-established circuit boards and conventions for plugging in those ICs. The JavaBeans-related notification mechanisms in this section and the next are a good start. Admittedly, as an industry and as professional software designers, we have a ways to go before the vision of true "software ICs and circuit boards" becomes a day-to-day reality.

So, for now, take a look at one Beans notification mechanism, called source-support-listener.

JDK 1.1 introduced property-change sources, property-change supports, and property-change listeners. Consider the sketch in Figure 5-36.

Hey, this looks rather familiar, doesn't it? In fact, it looks just like the sketch for observable components, from earlier in this chapter (Figure 5-17). So what's the difference you get with source-support-listener? The design is different. And what you supply is different. Take a look at the designs, side-by-side (Figure 5-37).

That which is above the dashed line comes from the *java.beans* class library; that which is below the dashed line is what you design and build.

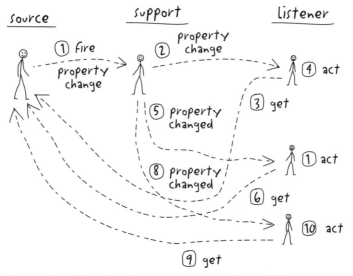

Figure 5-36.   Property-change source, support, and listener.

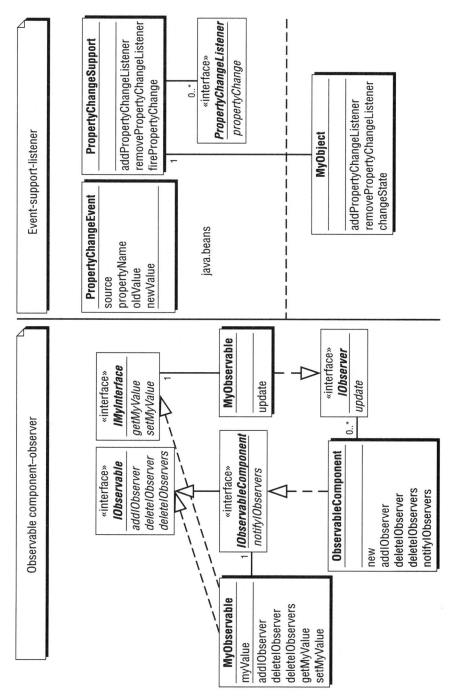

Figure 5-37. Comparing observable component–observer and event-support-listener.

271

You've seen the design on the left; take a look at the design on the right. The design within *java.beans* delivers quite a bit of functionality, a real help. You can use the PropertyChangeEvent class as is; there is no need to specialize it. The PropertyChangeSupport class is also ready to use as is; it includes its own notification mechanism. The PropertyChangeListener interface is ready to use; there's no need to extend it.

Okay, so now compare and contrast the two designs. Both designs use composition and delegation. The "observable component" design lets you plug in any notification mechanism you choose to use (flexible), yet you must supply it yourself (bummer).

The "source-support-listener" design supplies one notification mechanism (a good thing) yet fails to allow you to plug in your own notification mechanism instead (ugh!).

The scenario follows the same basic pattern as for the observable component (Figure 5-38).

The design lends itself to just one notification mechanism, using inheritance rather than composition.

Sounds like a perfect time for a teaching point and an improved design! The teaching point is "use a plug-in point (an interface) at those points you anticipate that others are likely to want flexibility."

So, for better flexibility over time, improve the design this way:

- Add two interfaces: IPropertyChangeSupport, IPropertyChangeSupportComponent.

- Let the default PropertyChangeSupport class implement the IPropertyChangeSupportComponent interface.

- Let MyObject hold an implementer of IPropertyChangeSupportComponent.

For example; see Figure 5-39.

Ahh, much better!

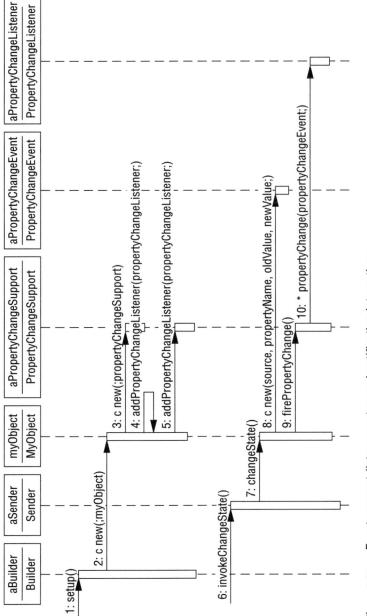

Figure 5-38. Event-support-listener: setup and notification interactions.

273

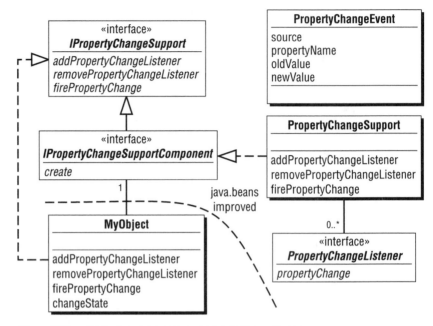

Figure 5-39.   An improved event-support-listener design.

For the first design, here's a Java snippet for a MyObject object and the PropertyChangeSupport object it holds:

```
public class MyObject {
✂
  private String name;
  private PropertyChangeSupport myPropertyChangeSupport;
  public void setName(String aName) {
    this.name = aName;
    myPropertyChangeSupport.firePropertyChange(propertyName, oldValue,
    newValue);
  }
✂
}
```

For the second design, here's a Java snippet for a MyObject object and the IPropertyChangeSupportComponent object it holds:

```
public class MyObject {

  private String name;
  private IPropertyChangeSupport myPropertyChangeSupport;
  public void setName(String aName) {
    this.name = aName;
    myPropertyChangeSupport.firePropertyChange(propertyName, oldValue,
    newValue);
  }

}


public interface IPropertyChangeSupport {
  void addPropertyChangeListener
    (PropertyChangeListener listener);
  void firePropertyChange(String propertyName,
    Object oldValue, Object newValue);
  void removePropertyChangeListener
    (PropertyChangeListener listener);
}


public interface IPropertyChangeSupportComponent
  extends IPropertyChangeSupport {
    IPropertyChangeSupport create ();
}
```

So when might you apply source-support-listener? Use it when
problem-domain objects need to notify user-interface objects. And
consider using it when one subsystem needs to notify other subsystems (the notification approach applies, even though JavaBeans itself does not support distributed listeners).

5.3.4   Producer-Bus-Consumer (InfoBus-Style Notification)

Producer-bus-consumer is a dataflow-oriented architecture for connecting objects and communicating between those objects.

Here's how it works:

1. A builder connects producers and consumers to a bus.

2. When a producer has data, he notifies the bus; the bus notifies all of its connected consumers.

3. If a consumer is interested in that data, he notifies the bus that he is interested in what that particular producer is producing; the bus notifies that producer.

4. That producer sends data, via the bus, to corresponding consumers.

5. Consumers can opt to sign up for future update notification from that producer.

For example, see Figures 5-40 and 5-41.

If you agree to implement certain interfaces and abide by the corresponding expectations about those interfaces, then you get a consistent way to plug-in producers and consumers without needing to handcraft the event-response interaction mechanism between them.

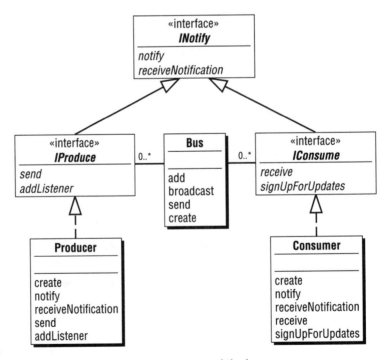

Figure 5-40.   Producers, consumers, and the bus.

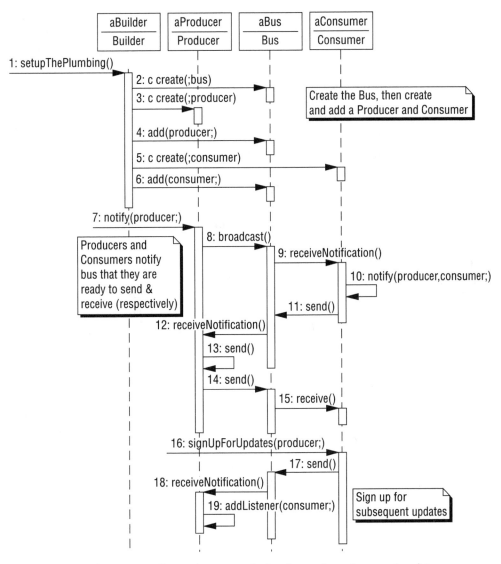

Figure 5-41.   Connect; communicate; sign up for subsequent updates.

Note that this is really all about plumbing, not content. The producer-bus-consumer architecture lets you plug in producers and consumers and get data to flow between them. Yet the structure and content of the data itself is application-specific, something you design-in yourself.

One example of producer-bus-consumer is called InfoBus. InfoBus is a better-organized way to approach JavaBean interaction, meaning it's a step above bean-by-bean connecting and communicating.

An InfoBus provides a data flow channel, connecting data producer(s) to data consumer(s).

To use the InfoBus approach, you must design producers and consumers that abide by certain conventions.

Producer and consumer objects must abide by *connecting convention,* for connecting to an InfoBus object. Any object in a class that implements InfoBusMember can connect to an InfoBus object.

Producer and consumer objects must follow a *communicating convention,* for communicating to another object via an InfoBus object. For objects you'd like to connect to the bus, the corresponding class must implement the InfoBusDataProducer interface, the InfoBusDataConsumer interface, or both. Then objects can indeed produce, consume, (as a producer) announce that something is ready, and then deliver it upon request, or (as a consumer) register for subsequent changes as a DataItemChangeListener.

Finally, it's up to you to design the *structure and content* of what you want to send from producer to consumer. To help with the structure side of the equation, InfoBus defines interfaces for ImmediateAccess (simple value interface) and RowSetAccess (row and column interface).

So when might you apply producer-bus? Some use this architecture to pass commands from a user query component to a database access component to a spreadsheet component. Okay, it's helpful yet not all that helpful.

When else might you use it? If you break up your design into subsystems with a dataflow interface between them, then yes this architecture makes sense. So:

- If you have an incoming telecommunication signal that you want to gradually refine with components that work on that incoming data stream . . .

- If you have a manufacturing system that monitors the flow of goods and products as it flows through the process . . .

- AND (in the case of InfoBus 1.1, at least) all of your components will run on one Java virtual machine (a current restriction, version 1.1). . . .

Then yes, producer-bus-consumer is for you.

5.3.5 Model-View-Controller (Swing-Style Notification)

Swing is part of the Java Foundation Classes (JFC) class library. It provides a more complete and polished set of GUI classes than those in the Abstract Window Toolkit (AWT) do.

AWT classes link to components on a native operating system.

Swing provides more than that, including pluggable look-and-feel (although few developers will directly work with it, it's nice to know it's there) and a lightweight component architecture.

Swing components use the model-view-controller notification mechanism. A "model" object is responsible for the concept that is being displayed or manipulated. A "view" object is responsible for displaying some aspect of this concept on a user's screen. Finally a "controller" object is responsible for handling input from the user and then sending that input to the appropriate methods of the view or model objects with which it is associated.

Swing implements model-view-controller this way. It defines a component class that establishes the model for a GUI widget. For example, it defines JButton as a kind of JComponent. JButton defines what operations and events apply to a button, including press, release, select, enable, and disable. JButton is indeed a model: It captures what a button is, regardless of how it is rendered in a window (something a view object can do) or detecting a user action on that button (something a controller object can do). The view and controller objects are implemented by different sub-packages of swing and give the button object its distinctive "look and feel" on the different platforms that the Java Virtual Machine runs on. In fact, for JButton the view and controller is combined into one class.

Here's an example. The class used for the Windows platform is com.sun.java.swing.plaf.windows.WindowsButtonUI. This class, just like other view-controllers for JButton, implements the ButtonUI interface. Plug in an object from a class that implements that interface and you're ready to go. Pluggable!

In fact, if you want to include a switchable UI feature within your app, you could select which set of view-controller classes will be used with the Swing components, like so:

```
try {UIManager.setLookAndFeel (
  "com.sun.java.swing.plaf.mac.MacLookAndFeel");}
catch (java.lang.ClassNotFoundException e {
  /* Can't find the look and feel factory class for Mac*/ }
```

This selects Mac look and feel and will give a Mac user interface even if your app is running on some other operating system.

Swing includes some more complex components. JTree is an example. JTree is a component that revolves around a model of objects arranged hierarchically. A JTree object consists of TreeNode objects; each TreeNode object has at most one parent; each TreeNode has some number of (0 or more) children. Actually, TreeNode is an interface; it includes the method signatures getParent(), children()-returns an Enumeration of children, isLeaf(), and getChildAt(int index). Swing also includes a TreeNode implementer, Default-MutableTreeNode, so that you can populate a tree of objects from your problem domain and get JTree to display the result.

An example? How about this. Charlie adds departments within his organization. He'd like to track his department hierarchy. The class diagram looks like Figure 5-42.

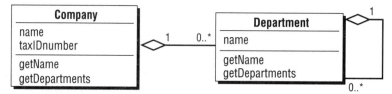

Figure 5-42. Charlie's empire expands.

And the Java code using Swing's JTree looks like this:

```
✂
//Create the nodes.
  DefaultMutableTreeNode top = new DefaultMutableTreeNode(company.get
    Name);
  Enumeration children = company.getDepartments();
  Department dept;

  while(children.hasMoreElements())
  {
    dept = (Department)children.nextElement();
    top.add(new DefaultMutableTreeNode(dept.getName()));
  }
//Create a tree.
  JTree tree = new JTree(top);
✂
```

This code uses DefaultMutableTreeNode, one of the family of classes and interfaces that define the model (as in model-view-controller) for the JTree component.

You could tie in your problem-domain methods more directly by adapting working with and providing adapters to another JTree companion interface, TreeModel. This interface includes these method signatures:

```
getChild(Object parent, int index)
getChildCount(Object parent)
getIndexOfChild(Object parent, Object child)
Object getRoot()
isLeaf(Object node)
```

Use an adapter class to implement those method signatures in terms of problem-domain methods. Pass an adapter-class instance to JTree, using its setModel(TreeModel model) method. And then let JTree interact directly via the adapter with the corresponding problem-domain hierarchy.

Important point: model-view pairs often swing together (bad pun intended). For example:

A problem-domain object (model) notifies . . .

A Swing model (acting as a view and controller for the problem-domain object)

Then that same Swing model notifies . . .

A Swing view and controller (a view and controller for the Swing model object).

5.3.6   Source-Distributed Listeners (Enterprise JavaBeans-Style Notification)

Enterprise JavaBeans (EJB) is a framework for building multi-tier distributed systems without so much pain and suffering. When implemented by vendors, it will include the infrastructure for transaction integrity (simple transactions, then later nested transactions) and state management across a network.

The spec includes both session objects and entity objects. Session objects encapsulate a client's state during a session. Entity objects have names, are locatable across the network, can service multiple clients across a network, and are persistent.

And the IBM San Francisco project is moving its results so they work within the EJB framework.

The Enterprise JavaBeans framework builds upon a number of core services:

- Java Transaction Service (JTS)
- Java Management API (JMAPI)
- Java Database Connectivity (JDBC)
- Java Message Service (JMS)

EJB hides a number of the core services, such as JTS and JDBC, from the application developer. Yet it makes JMS available to the application developer. And that's a good thing, since JMS is very useful for implementing message-based systems and distributed notification frameworks.

Note that EJB does *not* define a distributed implementation of the JavaBeans event model. One could use JMS to implement such a distributed event framework; even better: the messaging could be hidden within JavaBeans (yet it is not, at present).

The JMS describes a set of interfaces behind which many different implementations could be provided. A JMS provider is an implementation of the JMS using a particular messaging product. One could implement JMS over messaging middleware or over an ORB Event Service. JMS does not define the transport layer that an implementation should use.

The JMS architecture also includes:

- Clients, which send and receive messages
- Messages, defined by the application to pass information between clients
- Administered objects, pre-configured JMS objects, ready for clients to use.

JMS defines two distinct flavors of message systems: point-to-point and publish-subscribe. Both flavors specialize the following interfaces:

- ConnectionFactory, to create connections
- Connection, an active connection to a JMS Provider
- Destination, to identify a message destination
- Session, associated with a single thread context, used by
- MessageProducer and MessageConsumer, for sending and receiving messages.

Here's how to work with all this:

1. Set up the message infrastructure using ConnectionFactory and Destination. The point-to-point system uses Queue (a kind of Destination). The publish-subscribe system uses Topic (another kind of Destination).

2. Locate those objects using the Java Naming and Directory Interface (JNDI).

3. Use the connection factory to create connections.

4. Use connection objects to create session objects.

5. Using the session and destination objects, create message producers and message consumers.

6. Finally, at long last: pass JMS messages between clients.

For good measure, here is some example code for a client, using point-to-point messaging:

✂

```
//Get the JNDI object. This is where Administered Objects are registered
Context aContext = new InitialContext();

//We need a ConnectionFactory which in point to point
//is a QueueConnectionFactory
QueueConnectionFactory aQueueConnectionFactory;

// Now lookup the Queue Factory from JNDI
//The name would be configured by an administrator or
//by the JMS Provider installation
aQueueConnectionFactory =
(QueueConnectionFactory)aContext.lookup("ourQueueConnectionFactory");

//Now we need a Destination which in point to point is a Queue
Queue aQueue;

//To initialize we do another lookup for an Administrator provided Queue
aQueue = aContext.lookup("ourInterestingQueue");

//Now we create a Connection which in point to point
//is a QueueConnection
QueueConnection aQueueConnection;

//Initialize using the QueueConnectionFactory
aQueueConnection = aQueueConnectionFactory.createQueueConnection();
```

```
//Now we need a Session which in point to point
//is a QueueSession
QueueSession aQueueSession;

//Initialize using the Connection
aQueueSession =
aQueueConnection.createQueueSession
    (FALSE, Session.AUTO_ACKNOWLEDGE);

//To send and receive we need MessageProducers and MessageConsumers
//which in point to point are QueueSender and QueueReceiver
QueueSender aQueueSender;
QueueReceiver aQueueReceiver;

//Initialize using the Session and Destination
aQueueSender = aQueueSession.createSender(aQueue);
aQueueReceiver = aQueueSession.createReceiver(aQueue);

//An InterestingMessage type has been defined in the application
//Details omitted
```
✀
```
//Sending and Receiving a message

//Sending a Message
InterestingMessage anInterestingMessage = //initialization omitted
aQueueSender.send(anInteresingMessage);
```
✀
```
//Receiving a Mesage
InterestingMessage myInterestingMessage = aQueueReceiver.receive();
```
✀

The EJB story is evolving. We will continue to work out in practice
and then write about its impact on distributed Java design.

5.4 Summary

In this chapter, you've worked with notification and how it lets
other objects know that something significant has happened.

Passive notification is simple but resource intensive. Timer-based notification is a useful pattern. Active notification is most interesting; it's an essential ingredient for problem-domain object reuse; it's an essential ingredient for designing loosely coupled subsystems.

You've explored three major notification mechanisms:

- Passive: someone asks me if I've changed
- Timer-based: someone wakes me up
- Active: a source notifies its listeners (and the many variations on this theme)

The strategies you learned and applied in this chapter are:

Holder-Interface Strategy: *Establish a collection; define an interface.*

Balanced Design Strategy: *Design at two extremes and then somewhere in between. Design connotes looking at alternatives and picking a reasonable approach.*

Extracting Interfaces from a Class Hierarchy Strategy: *When you find that a subclass is inheriting one or more methods that are merely method signatures, use an interface for those method signatures. (That's exactly what an interface is for.)*

Don't Limit Your Interfaces with Needless Assumptions Strategy: *Consider typing your interface parameters as a built-in type (for example: int, float, String, StringBuffer, Object). Let each implementer of that interface test for the specific classes of objects it works with. Reason why: to increase the likelihood of reuse of each interface.*

Message Inward, Notify Outward Strategy:

     UI-invoked changes: message inward from UI to PD.

     PD-invoked changes: notify outward from PD to UI.

Repeater Strategy: *Use a repeater when you need to build a standard list of observers, so you can change observables and still use that standard list as is.*

Have *fun* with Java design!

Appendix A

Design Strategies

1.   Design by Example

Identify the Purpose Strategy: State the purpose of the system in 25 words or less.

Identify the Features Strategy: List the features for setting up, conducting the business, and assessing business results.

Select the Classes Strategy: Feature by feature, look for: role-player, role, transaction (moment or interval), place, container, or catalog-like description. For real-time systems, also look for data acquisition and control devices.

UI Content Strategy: Feature by feature, establish content: selections, lists, entry fields, display fields, actions, assessments.

High-Value Scenarios Strategy: Build scenarios that will exercise each "conducting business" and "assessing results" feature.

Action Sentence Strategy: Describe the action in a complete sentence. Put the action in the object (person, place, or thing) that has the "what I know" and "who I know" to get the job done.

Build a Class Diagram Strategy:

Start with scenario classes and methods.

Add attributes

Add associations—message paths for methods.

Add associations—look-up paths for the UI.

2.   Design with Composition, Rather than Inheritance

Composition Strategy: Use Composition to extend responsibilities by delegating work to other objects.

When to Inherit Strategy: Inheritance is used to extend attributes and methods; but encapsulation is weak within a class hierarchy, so use of this mechanism is limited. Use it when you can satisfy the following criteria:

1. *"Is a special kind of," not "is a role played by a"*

2. *Never needs to transmute to be an object in some other class*

3. *Extends rather than overrides or nullifies superclass*

4. *Does not subclass what is merely a utility class (useful functionality you'd like to reuse)*

5. *Within PD: expresses special kinds of roles, transactions, or things*

3.   Design with Interfaces

Challenge Each Association Strategy: Is this association hardwired only to objects in that class (simpler), or is this an association to any object that implements a certain interface (more flexible, extensible, pluggable)?

Challenge Each Message-Send Strategy: *Is this message-send hardwired only to objects in that class (simpler), or is this a message-send to any object that implements a certain interface (more flexible, extensible, pluggable)?*

Factor Out Repeaters Strategy: *Factor out method signatures that repeat within your class diagram. Resolve synonyms into a single signature. Generalize overly specific names into a single signature. Reasons for use: to explicitly capture the common, reusable behavior and to bring a higher level of abstraction into the model.*

Factor Out to a Proxy Strategy: *Factor out method signatures into a proxy, an object with a solo association to some other object. Reason for use: to simplify the proxy within a class diagram and its scenarios.*

Factor Out for Analogous Apps Strategy: *Factor out method signatures that could be applicable in analogous apps. Reason for use: to increase likelihood of using and reusing off-the-shelf classes.*

Factor Out for Future Expansion Strategy: *Factor out method signatures now, so objects from different classes can be graciously accommodated in the future. Reason for use: to embrace change flexibility.*

Where to Add Interfaces Strategy: *Add interfaces at those points in your design that you anticipate change: (1) Connect with an interface implementer rather than with an object in a specific class; (2) Send a message to an interface implementer rather than to an object in a specific class; and (3) Invoke a plug-in method rather than a method defined within a class.*

Design-in, from Features to Interfaces Strategy:

1. *Look for a common feature, one you need to provide in different contexts.*

2. *Identify a set of method names that correspond to that feature.*

3. *Add an interface.*

4. *Identify implementers.*

Design-in, from Role Doubles to Interfaces Strategy:

1. *Take a role and turn its method signatures into a role-inspired interface.*

2. *Let another role (a "role double") offer that same interface by:*

   - *implementing that interface, and*

   - *delegating the real work back to the original role player.*

Design-in, from Collections and Members to Interfaces Strategy:

1. *Does your object hold a collection of other objects? If so:*

   a. *Consider the potential "across the collection" method signatures.*

   b. *If other collections might offer the same set of method signatures, then design in that common interface.*

2. *Is your object a member within a collection? If so:*

   If that object needs to provide an interface similar to the collections it is in, then design in that common interface.

3. *Identify implementers.*

Design-in, from Scenarios to Interfaces Strategy:

1. *Look for similar interactions.*

2. *Add an interface-implementer column.*

   Use this naming convention:

   I<what it does> Implementer.

3. *Add an interface: I<what it does>.*

4. *Identify implementers.*

Interface Granularity Strategy: *If a method signature can only exist with others, then add it directly to an interface definition with those others (no need for a separate, one-signature interface).*

Design-in, from Intra-Class Roles to Interfaces Strategy:

1. *Identify roles that objects within a class can play.*

2. *Establish an interface for each of those roles.*

3. *Identify implementers.*

When to Use Plug-in Algorithms and Interfaces Strategy: *Use a plug-in algorithm and interface when you find this combination of problems:*

- *An algorithm you want to use can vary from object to object within a single class*

- *An algorithm is complex enough that you cannot drive its variation using attribute values alone.*

- *An algorithm is different for different categories of objects within a class—and even within those categories (hence, adding a category-description class won't resolve this problem).*

- *An algorithm you want to use will be different over time and you don't know at this point what all those differences will be.*

Design-in, from Plug-in Algorithms to Interfaces Strategy:

1. *Look for useful functionality you'd like to "plug in."*

2. *Add a plug-in point, using an interface.*

3. *Identify implementers.*

4. Design with Threads

Sync Access to Values Strategy: *When multiple threads compete for values(s) within an object—and you try other thread paths but cannot avoid competition for these values—use sync'd methods to limit access (one thread at a time). For multithreaded objects, sync each method that compares, operates on, gets, or sets internal values.*

Zoom In and Sync Strategy: *Zoom in on exactly what you need to sync, factor it out into a separate method, and sync that method. Why? Sync for as little time as possible so other (potentially higher priority) threads waiting at the start of other sync methods for that object will get to run sooner rather than later.*

Sync Access to Objects Strategy: *When multiple threads compete for entry into each other's sync'd methods, use a gatekeeper to control access one thread at a time, and make sure the objects that the gatekeeper protects have no sync methods.*

Value Gatekeeper Strategy: *Look for a method that increments or decrements a count of a limited resource. Sync that method; give it exclusive access to that count.*

Object Gatekeeper Strategy: *Look for a method that reserves or issues a limited resource, represented by the objects in that collection. Sync that method and give it exclusive access to that collection of objects.*

Four Thread Designs Strategy: *Apply these thread designs, looking for the simplest one that will satisfy your performance requirements. From simplest to most complex, consider: (1) single thread, (2) prioritized-object threads, (3) prioritized-method threads, (4) prioritized-method prioritized-object threads.*

Prioritized-Methods Strategy: *Prioritize your methods. Separate out cohesive functions with different priorities. Run higher priority methods in higher priority threads; run lower priority methods in lower priority threads.*

Thread Count Strategy: *Justify the existence of each thread in your design. If you can reduce the thread count and meet response time requirements, do so.*

5.   Design with Notification

Holder-Interface Strategy: *Establish a collection; define an interface.*

Balanced Design Strategy: *Design at two extremes and then some- where in between. Design connotes looking at alternatives and picking a reasonable approach.*

Extracting Interfaces from a Class Hierarchy Strategy: *When you find that a subclass is inheriting one or more methods that are merely method signatures, use an interface for those method signatures. (That's exactly what an interface is for.)*

Don't Limit Your Interfaces with Needless Assumptions Strategy: *Consider typ- ing your interface parameters as a built-in type (for example: int, float, String, StringBuffer, Object). Let each implementer of that interface test for the specific classes of objects it works with. Reason why: to increase the likelihood of reuse of each interface.*

Message Inward, Notify Outward Strategy:

UI-invoked changes: message inward from UI to PD.

PD-invoked changes: notify outward from PD to UI.

Repeater Strategy: *Use a repeater when you need to build a stan- dard list of observers, so you can change observables and still use that standard list as is.*

Appendix B

Notation Summary

Here is a convenient notation summary, a subset of Unified Modeling Language (UML 1.2):

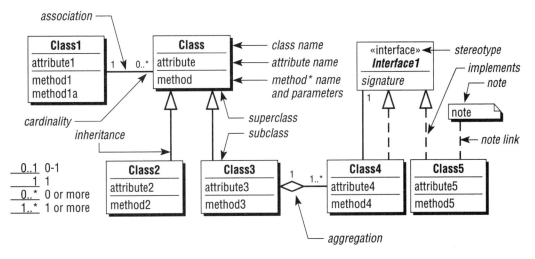

Figure B-1. Class diagram notation.

---

*What Java calls a method, UML calls an operation. This book uses the Java name for this concept.

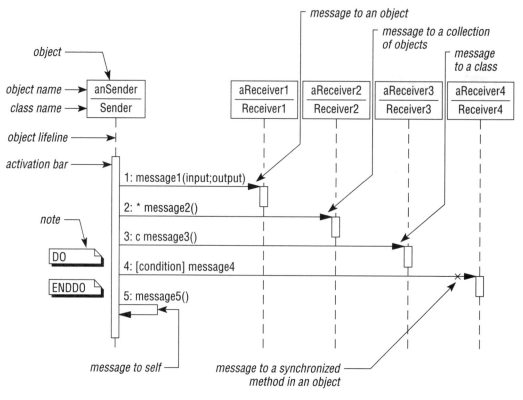

Figure B-2. Sequence-diagram notation.

Note: This notation is based on UML 1.2, with compatible extensions for multiple outputs, class messages, and messages to synchronized methods.

Appendix C

Java Visibility

The Java programming language includes public, protected, default, and private visibility.

Figure C-1 presents a concise summary.

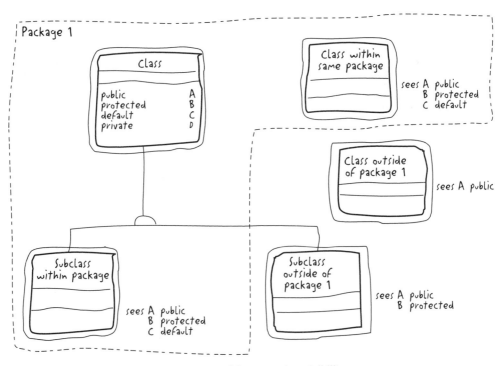

Figure C-1. A summary of Java scoping visibility.

Bibliography

[CoadLetter] Coad, Peter, *The Coad Letter.*
http://www.oi.com/publications.htm

> *The Coad Letter* is a technical newsletter. It features new advances in building object models. Delivered exclusively by e-mail. Free.

[Coad97] Coad, Peter, with David North and Mark Mayfield, *Object Models: Strategies, Patterns and Applications,* 2nd ed. Englewood Cliffs, N.J.: Prentice Hall, 1997.

> This teaches how to build better object models (3 business apps, 2 real-time apps; 177 strategies, 31 patterns; key results in Coad, OMT, and UML notations).

Cornell, Gary and Horstmann, Cay, *Core Java 1.1 Fundamentals* and *Core Java 1.1:Advanced Features,* Englewood Cliffs, N.J.: Prentice Hall, 1997.

> This pair of programming books have a good blend of illustrations and source code. The second includes quite a bit of material on threads.

Flanagan, David, *Java in a Nutshell,* 2nd ed. Sebastopol, CA: O'Reilly & Associates, 1997.

> This programming book is source-code intensive. There are few illustrations although it includes lots of well-commented Java code.

[Gamma 95] Gamma, Erich, Richard Helm, Ralph Johnson, and John Vlissides, *Design Patterns,* Reading, MA: Addison-Wesley, 1995.

   This book details many useful patterns, including factory, strategy, and observer patterns.

Index

THE SOFTWARE INCLUDED ON THIS CD WILL
HELP YOU REALLY **MASTER** JAVA DESIGN!

We wanted to deliver more than just a book. You see, no matter
how good any book is, nothing replaces the added understanding
and insights that come from hands-on experience. So to help you
get the most out of your Java design experience, to make it more
hands-on and more effective, we've put together this special *Java
Design* CD. It features:

- Together/J Whiteboard Edition (no time limits, no size limits)

- Complete source code for the examples in this book

- Runnable demos (console apps and GUIs)

- Complete HTML documentation for the software, source code,
  and demos

- Java design strategies in HTML

Buy the book. Start reading. Install the software and take it for a
spin. View and edit the source code using TJ's *simultaneous*
round-trip engineering. View the sequence diagrams too. Keep
reading. And applying.

THEN use your new Java design skills and the software to design
and build better apps. You're on your way!

THIS IS A MULTIPLATFORM CD
Use it on Windows 95/98, NT, Solaris, Linux, and OS/2.

FOR MORE INFORMATION
Visit <http://www.oi.com/>www.oi.com   *or*
    <http://www.togetherj.com/>www.togetherj.com